The FairTax Book

The FairTax Book

Saying Goodbye to the Income Tax and the IRS*

*Not to mention the Social Security tax, the Medicare tax, corporate income taxes, the death tax, the self-employment tax, the alternative minimum tax, the gift tax, capital gains taxes, tax audits, and some major headaches every April 15.

NEAL BOORTZ

& CONGRESSMAN JOHN LINDER

HARPER

NEW YORK · LONDON · TORONTO · SYDNEY

A hardcover edition of this book was published in 2005 by HarperCollins Publishers.

THE FAIRTAX BOOK. Copyright © 2005 by Neal Boortz and John Linder. All rights reserved. Printed in the United States of America. No part of this book may be used or reproduced in any manner whatsoever without written permission except in the case of brief quotations embodied in critical articles and reviews. For information, address HarperCollins Publishers Inc., 10 East 53rd Street, New York, NY 10022.

HarperCollins books may be purchased for educational, business, or sales promotional use. For information please write: Special Markets Department, HarperCollins Publishers Inc., 10 East 53rd Street, New York, NY 10022.

FIRST PAPERBACK EDITION PUBLISHED 2006.

Designer: Publications Development Company of Texas

The Library of Congress has cataloged the hardcover edition as follows:

Boortz, Neal.
  The FairTax book : saying goodbye to the income tax and the IRS / Neal Boortz & John Linder.—1st ed.
xx, 188 p. : ill. ; 22 cm.
0-06-087541-0 (alk. paper)

2005452176

HJ4652.B65 2005

ISBN 13: 978-0-06-087549-7 (pbk.)
ISBN 10: 0-06-087549-6 (pbk.)

08 09 10 PDC/RRD 20

This book is dedicated to the tens of thousands of Americans—individuals and business owners alike—who have found their dreams of a better life crushed under the weight of an oppressive tax system that stifles initiative and punishes achievement.

CONTENTS

CONTENTS

PREFACE

Yes, we know. This book seems rather short. It's not three hundred pages long. Well, that's exactly as it should be. So take it to the cash register and buy it anyway.

This is a book about liberation. It's a book about replacing personal and corporate income taxes, death taxes, payroll taxes, capital gains taxes, self-employment taxes—all of those wonderful taxes that thrill you so much year after year—with one tax: a consumption tax collected only when you choose to spend your hard-earned money at the retail level. This book is about a 133-page tax reform bill currently before the House Ways and Means Committee that will replace more than sixty thousand pages of IRS rules and regulation with an easy-to-comprehend national retail sales tax. The idea is simple, easy to understand, workable, and, above all, fair. It will revolutionize the American economy and begin a new wave of freedom around the globe.

The idea is so simple, and so good, that we felt this book wouldn't *have* to be long. We figure it won't take you three hundred pages to feel the same way.

A WORD FROM CONGRESSMAN JOHN LINDER

I have known Neal Boortz for thirty-five years. I knew him when he was poor. (He no longer is!) I knew him when his federal income tax liability was barely four figures. Today it is considerably larger. I knew him when he could do his own taxes in one evening. This year he paid for his accountant's new luxury car.

For twenty-five of those thirty-five years, we've talked about the failure of our income tax system. We've agreed that our tax system crushes entrepreneurship, punishes achievement, and discourages capital formation. We've both lamented the fact that our federal income tax has become the single largest contributor to job loss and capital flight. And we've talked about replacing our income tax system with a national sales tax.

Adam Smith said that the invisible hand of the economy creates efficient markets. That is true. It is also true that the IRS is the lead foot on the throat of our economy.

It's time for the American people to pull that foot off.

I first introduced the FairTax Bill (H.R. 25) in July 1999. It has been reintroduced in each Congress. In the most recent Congress, we had fifty-four cosponsors. Whenever Neal mentions it on his nationally syndicated talk radio show, it ties up the lines for hours—often into the next day. On this issue, we both believe that the public is way ahead of the politicians. The people are ready. *You* are ready.

Our collaboration on this book has been challenging and fun. The inflammatory and rude references come from Neal. That's just the way he is. I, of course, provided the intellectual backdrop that allows him to be outrageous. Just call me the straight man.

We hope you find this book both informative and entertaining. I'll take full credit for the informative content. Neal can take the heat on the entertainment value.

John Linder
United States Congressman

A WORD FROM NEAL BOORTZ

You've just picked up a book about taxes. What in the world are you thinking?

Don't you want to read something a bit more entertaining? Something with a few gratuitous sex scenes? I've never written a sex scene. Perhaps you'd feel a little better if I put one in the prologue. We could start with a little something about how Americans have been getting screwed by the current tax system for decades.

You might even be thinking you'd rather be watching a nice reality show instead of reading a book about (yawn!) taxes.

If it's reality you want, take a good hard look at your next paycheck.

In fact, I insist that you do so. Right now. Go get that pay stub and start adding up the amounts the government has deducted—for federal income taxes, Social Security taxes, and Medicare taxes. Now figure out what percentage of your paycheck is gone. Keep that percentage in mind. It will lead to clarity of thought as you read on.

We'll admit that the subject of taxes is dull. Not so dull when you're being audited, maybe, but dull enough. Think hard about how many really interesting accountants you've known. See what we mean? The subject may be dull, but John Linder and I have worked hard to make certain this book isn't. If I've accomplished nothing else during my thirty-five-plus years of hosting a talk radio show, I like to think at least I've learned how to take the most mundane, dreary, mind-numbing subjects and turn them into compelling radio programming. I could keep you glued to a radio for hours talking about sewing neckties if I put my mind to it. I once did an entire show on the efficacy of a liberal arts education in a largely technological society. I should have nabbed a Nobel Prize for that one. The idea for the show came from somewhere else, but I took it and made people listen.

So here's our promise: Now that you've spent a few bucks to buy this book (we figure you did that after reading the Preface), take it home and read it. Read it twice if you have to. When you finish, we believe you'll be convinced—and motivated. You'll be so ready for the FairTax to be passed that you'll start camping on your congressman's or senator's doorstep until you get a personal audience. You'll pass this book on to your friends and coworkers, accompanied by dire threats of the loss of your friendship if they don't start joining you in those doorstep camping expeditions.

This book is about transforming a nation. It is about taking one of the most hated institutions in American life—the Internal Revenue Service—and sending it to that place in the government guano heap of history it has so richly earned. More important, this book is about your personal financial liberation and independence. It's about your getting 100 percent of your paycheck every second Friday. It's about being able to save and invest, for your future and for the future of your nation's economy, without worrying one moment about the tax consequences. It's about an economy growing so fast that you'll have to hide under your bed to *avoid* a good job. It's about economic liberty. It's about making April 15 just another beautiful spring day, messed up by nothing more than pollen and its usual assault on your allergies.

You've no doubt heard about the FairTax by now. It's certainly on the political radar screen, and many politicians and others with an interest in keeping our current tax system in place seem awfully afraid of it. They're concerned . . . and that's good. We're sure you've heard some politician or pundit say that the FairTax would constitute a huge increase in the tax burden on poor and working families. They're wrong, and they know it. Read this book, and you'll know for certain that anyone who utters those words either (a) hasn't read the Fair-Tax Bill and knows only enough about this tax reform idea to be dangerous or (b) has decided to lie to you intentionally.

In the following pages, we'll start with a brief history of income taxation. You need to know the enemy and how it works in order to be prepared to vanquish it. And make no mistake: Our current tax system—no matter how friendly it may be to the dreams of politicians—is your dire enemy if you dream of financial independence. Our current tax system is one that punishes the behaviors Americans value and rewards the behaviors we abhor. Those in our society who work hard and achieve are punished with taxes that approach confiscatory levels. Eschew hard work, follow the path of least resistance, and your tax burden all but disappears while the taxpayer-funded government largesse pours in.

You'll also learn how politicians have managed to mold our tax code into an instrument designed not so much for raising revenue to fund the legitimate operations of government, as to control the behavior of individual Americans and corporations, and to give politicians levers to pull and buttons to push to buy votes when reelection time comes around.

This book is about one revolutionary piece of legislation that's designed to change all that: H.R. 25, the FairTax Plan. For more than twenty years, I have personally been a proponent of replacing our income tax with a consumption tax. John Linder has made it a focus of his career in Washington. And, as John mentioned, my listeners share my excitement; they've called by the thousands, wanting to know what they can do to support the FairTax movement. If I can get my listeners that excited with just a few words on the radio, think what we can do for you with an entire book.

Our goal here is twofold. First, we're going to turn you into a rabid warrior for tax reform. Second, in all honesty we wouldn't mind having the phrase "*New York Times* Bestselling Author" placed before our names. You can do your part by buying this book. We'll do our part as you read it.

Oh . . . and that thing about passing this book on to your friends? Forget it. Make them buy their own. The more of these books in circulation the better. Read this copy and lose it in an airport somewhere. Then go out and buy another copy—and find a good place to lose that one, too.

Stand by for America's Second Revolution.

Neal Boortz
Reformed Attorney
Host, *The Neal Boortz Show*

The FairTax Book

"Congress went beyond merely enacting an income tax law and repealed Article IV of the Bill of Rights, by empowering the tax collector to do the very things from which that article says we were to be secure. It opened up our homes, our papers and our effects to the prying eyes of government agents and set the stage for searches of our books and vaults and for inquiries into our private affairs whenever the tax men might decide, even though there might not be any justification beyond mere cynical suspicion.

"The income tax is bad because it has robbed you and me of the guarantee of privacy and the respect for our property that were given to us in Article IV of the Bill of Rights. This invasion is absolute and complete as far as the amount of tax that can be assessed is concerned. Please remember that under the Sixteenth Amendment, Congress can take 100 percent of our income anytime it wants to. As a matter of fact, right now it is imposing a tax as high as 91 percent. This is downright confiscation and cannot be defended on any other grounds.

"The income tax is bad because it was conceived in class hatred, is an instrument of vengeance and plays right into the hands of the communists. It employs the vicious communist principle of taking from each according to his accumulation of the fruits of his labor and giving to others according to their needs, regardless of whether those needs are the result of indolence or lack of pride, self-respect, personal dignity or other attributes of men.

"The income tax is fulfilling the Marxist prophecy that the surest way to destroy a capitalist society is by steeply graduated taxes on income and heavy levies upon the estates of people when they die.

"As matters now stand, if our children make the most of their capabilities and training, they will have to give most of it to the tax collector and so become slaves of the government. People cannot pull themselves up by the bootstraps anymore because the tax collector gets the boots and the straps as well.

"The income tax is bad because it is oppressive to all and discriminates particularly against those people who prove themselves most adept at keeping the wheels of business turning and creating maximum employment and a high standard of living for their fellow men.

"I believe that a better way to raise revenue not only can be found but must be found because I am convinced that the present system is leading us right back to the very tyranny from which those, who established this land of freedom, risked their lives, their fortunes and their sacred honor to forever free themselves. . . ."

> T. Coleman Andrews
> Commissioner of Internal Revenue,
> 1953–1955

INTRODUCTION

When Karl Marx wrote *The Communist Manifesto* in 1848, he included ten points—goals, if you will, that must be accomplished to bring about a true communist society. Number two on Marx's list was the establishment of "a heavy progressive or graduated income tax." Number three was the "abolition of all rights of inheritance."[1] It wasn't many years after Marx set forth these ten points that the progressive income tax became the goal of much of the American political and intellectual class. Eventually, this second most important of Marx's goals was accomplished—in the United States. (The death tax addressed Marx's third goal, though not completely.)

So it's no surprise that, at the height of the Cold War, a staunch anticommunist like T. Coleman Andrews would recognize that America must find a better way to raise revenue

---

1. We could point out that number ten on Marx's list was "Free education for all children in public schools." We are disinclined, however, to open that can of worms. We're here to talk taxes, not education.

than an income tax—despite (or perhaps because of) the fact that he'd just spent three years running the government agency charged with collecting that tax. Well, a better way *has* been found. It's called the FairTax, and you're about to learn all about it.

This is a book about taxes. It's also a book about economics. Perhaps the best thing we can say about this book is that it is about hope . . . tremendous hope. It's a book about things happening every day in our country, and what we can do to change them. Every day, jobs leave this country to go to lower wage markets overseas . . . and America suffers. Every day, domestic manufacturers shut their doors because cheaper goods are imported from across the oceans . . . and America suffers. Every day, individuals and businesses endure seemingly endless forms based on seemingly impossible rules simply so that they can pay their taxes honestly and accurately . . . and America suffers. There is a better way—a way filled with hope and promise for America's economic future—and it is called the FairTax.

Let's agree up front that this book is about honesty. And here comes an important step in establishing that honesty: This is not a book about tax cuts.

That's right. Do we want tax cuts and lower government spending? Absolutely. But that's a different book and a different fight. Tearing out the American tax code by its roots and replacing it with something simpler is a big enough challenge without trying to reform government and decrease government spending at the same time. So this book isn't about saving us a penny in taxes. We'll fight those battles later. First we have to fight for a simpler, clearer way to fund our federal government—a way that protects freedom, promotes individuality, and spawns economic growth.

If we agree that we're all in the hunt together for a better future for our families and our country, then we're all looking for the solutions to the same set of problems. In this book, we lay out a very thorough solution that goes a long way toward addressing our nation's economic ills. Before you embrace it enthusiastically—and we believe you will—we encourage you to read it critically . . . and ponder how together we can make the idea even better. We are already working aggressively with literally thousands of FairTax volunteers across the country to bring the FairTax to reality, but we need your help. Any progress we can make to rid ourselves of our current income tax code—a code that is dragging down our economy, discouraging achievement, and sometimes destroying families—will be an improvement.

This book is not a partisan effort. It's not about Republicans, Democrats, or Libertarians. It's not about liberals or conservatives. It's not about rich versus poor, black versus white, or citizen versus illegal immigrant. It's about revitalizing America's economy and nurturing the free enterprise soul of America that has made this the greatest country in the world in which to live, work, and play.

꩜

Before we walk you through the details of the FairTax, let us say a word about our plan for this book. It's going to involve a little education, but we'll try to make it as painless as possible.

First, we'll walk you through how we got here—how we came to be saddled with our incomprehensible and punishing tax code. This is important because it speaks directly to where we need to go from here.

Then we'll show you the government's two favorite tricks for distracting you from focusing on the actual amount of taxes you pay. The first is that neat little idea called "withholding." The tax withholding system has fooled many Americans into thinking of April 15 as refund day instead of tax day. We're all happy to crow about the size of our tax refunds, but how many of us can answer the simple question of how much tax we've actually paid? The second trick is the whole idea of business and corporate taxes. Many of our fellow citizens would like it just fine if we abolished personal taxes and placed the entire tax burden on business. As we'll show you, though, businesses don't *pay* taxes. They merely *collect* taxes—and then pass them on to you, the consumer. At the final accounting, the entire tax burden comes right back to the individual consumer. We'll show you why these business taxes, and our misconceptions about business, are costing us American jobs and American factories.

Next, we'll show you two of the biggest reasons your tax bill is as high as it is: tax evasion, and Social Security and Medicare. That's right: Whenever someone manages to dodge paying his or her full complement of taxes, someone else has to pick up the slack. That would be you. And when America's two largest social programs—Social Security and Medicare—sink into financial trouble, who else can the government turn to? Again, that would be you.

Then we'll explain the FairTax in detail. We'll show you how it deals with each of these issues fairly and efficiently. We'll walk you through the plan step by step, detailing both the good and the bad. There's an old saying in Washington: A good lobbyist will tell you everything good about his side of the issue, and then he'll tell you everything bad. If a lobbyist won't show you both sides, either he hasn't been well briefed, or he can't be trusted. We will work to earn your trust by giving you both sides of the story. No tax reform plan is perfect. But we believe the FairTax is about as close as you can get.

Questions? Well, we haven't heard them all . . . but we've sure heard most of them in our experiences with town hall meetings and talk radio shows. Before the end of the book, we'll try to answer all of the most frequently asked questions.

Objections? We've heard those, too. Some are valid. But others are based on a personal fear that the FairTax will destroy the questioner's lucrative career of gaming the present tax system for his personal benefit or that of his high-paying clients. We have nothing to hide here. We'll tell you what the naysayers are saying. We'll dissect their arguments to expose the misunderstandings, outright distortions, and whatever grains of truth there might be.

We've included a chapter about IRS outrages. We all have a little fear of this agency, and many of us have had bad experiences dealing with tax authorities. Our goal here isn't to place any blame on the men and women working for the IRS. The vast majority of them are just doing their jobs—jobs made very difficult by the laws passed by nearly a century of congresses and presidents. But the power concentrated in this agency is subject to abuse, and the odds are that you've seen or experienced some of that abuse firsthand. The FairTax is not a finger-pointing campaign aimed at the IRS. However, its goal *is* to eliminate the IRS—an event we believe will generate few tears among American taxpayers. We've included a chapter describing the IRS's record of performance to remind us of the atrocities and absurdities that can occur under our present system.

Finally, we'll conclude with a chapter on how you—that's right, *you*—can help. It's time to step away from the sidelines. The future of this debate and this country are in your hands; only you can convince your elected representatives that the FairTax needs to become a reality. The fact is, many elected representatives don't need convincing; they just need to be convinced of your approval. They can read the economic reports as well as anyone, but they also know that big ideas tend to scare people. Elected officials don't like to scare people. Scared people vote for someone else. Your congressmen and senators need you to call, to write, and to show up at town hall meetings and say, "It's okay. This is one big idea that doesn't scare us. We want you to move forward."

We don't expect everyone to agree with us on everything, but the problems facing our nation are real and require action. Our economy needs a boost. We need more well-paying jobs for Americans. We need to do something to keep American businesses at home. And we need to unleash, once more, the tremendous potential that has been all but suffocated for so long by a tax system that discourages the very things we need to bring these goals about.

As usual, the longer we wait, the more painful the solution will ultimately be. The time is right for the FairTax. The perfect storm is brewing to facilitate a change of this magnitude. Those who have made their lush livings playing the intricacies of our current tax code are concerned. J. Craig Shearman, vice president of government relations for the National Retail Federation—an organization on record as opposing the FairTax—recently said: "A year ago this was an idea being touted by one obscure congressman from Georgia. Six months ago it was an idea being touted by the majority leader of the House. Now it's an idea that is being talked about by the president of the United States."[2]

That "obscure congressman" goes by the name of John Linder. When you've finished this book, perhaps you'll join the effort to make the FairTax, and thus Congressman Linder, a little less obscure.

---

2. Quoted in "Baby Steps Taken on Tax Reform Chafe GOP," *Atlanta Journal-Constitution* (November 29, 2004), p. 1A.

1

THE HISTORY OF OUR INCOME TAX

No... you haven't bought a history book. You've bought a book that details a new method of raising revenue for the federal government that will send the American economy into warp drive—while restoring financial privacy and economic liberty to American families and wage earners.

To plan successfully for the future, though, it's necessary to have at least a basic understanding of the past. If we're trying to kill a bureaucratic monster that destroys initiative and impedes economic growth, it's crucial that we know just what cave that monster crawled out of. In the words of the American philosopher George Santayana, "Those who cannot remember the past are condemned to repeat it."

As you read this depressing (though brief) history of the income tax in America—and the chapter on withholding that follows—keep this basic fact in mind: There is absolutely no limit to the government's desire for your money. When it comes to politicians' powers of taxation, the only limit they recognize is the people's willingness to tolerate the confiscation of their wealth. The amount of your earnings that the government is willing to leave in your pocket is only the amount it cannot seize without promoting an outright rebellion.

In the early years of our republic, the federal government levied few taxes. The Feds managed to get by with only a handful: taxes on alcohol, carriages, and some basic consumer items such as sugar and tobacco. When the United States went to war against Great Britain in 1812, sales taxes were placed on various luxury items to cover the cost. The cost of fighting a war can be high, but citizens are generally amenable to higher taxes in times of war because they realize that the cost of not fighting the war can be even higher. These patriotic feelings would be exploited in later years to the immense benefit of the free-spending political class.

In 1817, with Great Britain once again defeated, Congress did away with all internal taxes and funded the cost of the federal government with tariffs on imports.

Remember, please, that during this period of American history most governing was done at the local, not the national, level. This is as our founding fathers wanted it. Various people present when our Constitution was drafted expressed a belief that, in times of peace, roughly 95 percent of all governing should be at the state and local levels, with the remaining 5 percent coming from the federal government. Add that to the list of founding principles that have been all but ignored.

The first attempt at an income tax came about to raise funds for what we know as the Civil War.[1] In 1861, Congress passed a bill assessing a 3 percent income tax on everyone earning between $600 and $10,000 a year. Six hundred dollars a year in 1861 would equal about $10,000 now. If you earned more than $10,000 (about $166,700 today), the rate went to 5 percent and a nice little inheritance tax was added to the mix, as were some additional sales and excise taxes.

The Union wasn't alone in enacting the income tax. The idea also caught hold south of the Mason-Dixon line, and the Confederate states enacted their own version. Misery, it seems, has always loved company.

By 1872, with the war over, the populace was starting to show its displeasure with the income tax. The political class reacted by eliminating the income tax. The Feds went back to taxing tobacco and booze. Yet the politicians' dreams of a permanent income tax weren't easy to squelch; the snake was hibernating, not dead. Over the next twenty years or more,

---

1. "Strictly speaking, there never was an American Civil War. A civil war is a conflict in which two or more factions fight for control of a nation's government. That was not the case in the United States between 1861 and 1865. The seceding Southern states were not trying to take over the U.S. government; they wanted to declare themselves independent." Thomas E. Woods, Ph.D., *The Politically Incorrect Guide to American History* (Regnery, 2004), p. 61.

members of Congress introduced no less than sixty-eight bills to enact another income tax.

The second term of President Grover Cleveland brought us the economic fiasco that's gone down in history as the Panic of 1893. First, the Reading Railroad (remember it from Monopoly?) went into receivership. A few banks and other businesses dependent on the railroad followed, and soon we had a general economic downturn. Now, as we've learned, when the economy goes sour that's a signal for the government to start taking more money out of the pockets of its citizens. It was time to try an income tax again.

Using the Panic as a handy excuse, eager politicians passed a law calling for a new income tax in 1894. Politicians then, as now, were not particularly eager to showcase just what they were trying to accomplish, so they made a blatant attempt to quell any possibility of a strong anti-income tax response from the voters by assigning a rather bizarre title to the new tax bill. They called it "An act to reduce taxation, to provide revenue for the government, and for other purposes."[2] Just how much can you trust a politician who passes a law to tax your income, and calls it an "act to reduce taxation"?

The 1894 "act to reduce taxation" presented Americans with a 2 percent tax on everyone making more than $4,000 a

---

2. The practice of assigning names to mask the true purpose of the legislation is a time-honored practice in Washington. There is a law on the books that authorizes the federal government to use banks to spy on your financial transactions. For instance, let's say you were to sell a car to someone for $10,000. Wary of fraud, you demanded and received cash for your car. If you were to deposit that

year (the equivalent of $50,000 today). In a nice twist, our politicians decided that all government officials—state and local alike—would be exempt from the new tax. Not a bad deal! Tax the people, exempt yourself. That's what the politicians of 1894 meant by "equal treatment under the law." Why not give it a try? Who knows . . . it just might have worked.[3]

As it turned out, this 2 percent tax on incomes over $4,000 started a chain of events that culminated in a constitutional amendment and our current income tax system. President Grover Cleveland, you see, thought that the 2 percent income tax was unconstitutional, so he let it become law without his signature. The question of constitutionality was presented to the U.S. Supreme Court—and the income tax lost.[4] The Supremes ruled that the income tax was actually a direct tax on the citizens of the United States, a violation of the Constitution.[5]

Now here's where things get really depressing. After an income tax was declared unconstitutional, the politicians in

---

cash into your checking account, your bank would be required to file a written report with the federal government detailing the transaction. You are not to be notified that your transaction has been reported. The name of the law? The Bank Secrecy Act.

3. Could there possibly be one person reading this who does not believe that our elected officials would not opt for a similar exclusion today if they thought they could get away with it?

4. Arthur Eckrich, "The Sixteenth Amendment: The Historical Background," *Cato Journal* (Spring 1981).

5. "No Capitation, or other direct, Tax shall be laid, unless in Proportion to the Census of Enumeration hereinbefore directed to be taken," *Article 1, Section 9: Constitution of the United States.*

Washington chose sides and drew their battle lines. On one hand we had Democrats, who were eager to spend the money that would come from an income tax. The Democrats called for a constitutional amendment permitting the income tax in both their 1896 and 1908 platforms. Republicans, on the other hand, were opposed to the idea in principle.

Those who favored the idea of an income tax met with considerable success, capturing public sentiment with promises that the tax would "soak the rich," and leave the vast majority of Americans alone. Economic class warfare was as alive and well in the early 1900s as it is in the early 2000s.

The historical timeline now brings us to Texas Senator Joseph Bailey, a conservative Democrat. Deciding to play the game of partisan politics, Bailey cooked up a scheme to humiliate congressional Republicans. Though he was opposed to the idea, Bailey introduced a bill calling for an income tax. He mistakenly thought that the Republicans would rush in to kill this legislation, thus furthering the image Democrats were trying to cultivate of Republicans as hostile to the poor and concerned only about protecting the wealthy. Wouldn't you know it, things didn't turn out as Bailey had planned. Liberal Republicans, backed by Teddy Roosevelt, actually came out in support of the bill. Passage seemed all but certain.

Conservative Republicans were panicked. They needed a way to derail the Bailey bill and the growing threat of an income tax. In one of the worst examples of legislative play-calling in our history, Republicans came up with the brilliant idea of announcing that they would support the idea of an income tax on one condition: if and only if it came about as the result of an amendment to our Constitution.

Even though this group of conservative Republicans felt that there was some slight chance the proposed amendment might actually make it through the House and the Senate, there was just no way in the world that the legislatures of three-fourths of the states could vote for ratification. Yeah . . . right.

Big oops.

The amendment sailed through the House and the Senate. The vote in the Senate was 77 to 0, and the House approved it by 318 to 14. It was off to the states for ratification. Conservative Republicans were still confident that the effort was doomed. They were as wrong as they could be.

Smelling ultimate victory for one of their long-held goals, the Democrats launched a massive effort to convince the people that any income tax would be directed only at the wealthy, and that ordinary Americans would be left virtually untaxed. Conservative legislatures in the West and the South convinced their constituents that the adoption of the income tax would have little effect on them, since incomes high enough to be taxed were rare in these areas. The people, thus anesthetized, raised little objection and the Sixteenth Amendment was ratified on February 12, 1913. This date should be added to December 7, 1941, and September 11, 2001, as dates in American history that shall forever live in infamy.

In the beginning, as advertised, the federal income tax was indeed a tax on the "evil and hated rich." When the income tax first arrived, only one-half of 1 percent of American income earners actually paid any income tax. In today's dollars, you would have had to have an income of $250,000 or more to feel the first 1 percent pinch; a 7 percent rate would kick in for those making more than the equivalent of $6 million a year.

It is not necessary for the purposes of this book to go into the gory and depressing details of how the tax burden on Americans has increased over the past ninety-plus years. Suffice it to say that those who felt the income tax would affect only the very wealthy were soon shocked into reality. The income tax soon became a burden not just to the wealthy, but to average American families struggling to raise their children and plan for retirement while somehow ending up with enough money left over to enjoy in their personal lives.

Today, this struggle is nearing a crisis point: the income tax is being molded into a more perfect weapon of class warfare. In 2003, the last year for which figures are available, the top 52 percent of all income earners paid virtually 100 percent of all personal income taxes collected by the Internal Revenue Service. We are just a few years away from the point where the majority of American wage earners will have no federal income tax liability at all. The purpose of this book is not to illustrate how our income tax is used as an instrument of class warfare. This might, however, be a good place to pause and reflect on what might transpire when politicians need the votes of the non-tax-paying majority more than the votes of the people actually covering the tab.

Not a comforting thought, is it?

Back to our history lesson: With the ratification of the Sixteenth Amendment, our politicians had finally realized their long-term goal of instituting an income tax. Yet they soon discovered, to their dismay, that there were limitations.

One problem was that the voters were determined to hold politicians to their promise that the tax would be levied only on the rich. Another problem was the method of payment. As we'll see in the next chapter, the voters rebelled against the idea of withholding tax. Tax bills were paid on an annual basis. Under those conditions, it's rather hard for politicians to raise tax rates or to expand the reach of the tax.

But another force would soon come along to give politicians the leverage they needed to turn the tax tide in their favor. That force was war.

2

... THEN CAME WITHHOLDING

Perhaps the best way to introduce the subject of withholding is to tell you just why politicians love the withholding system so much. It's really very simple: Politicians love withholding because it gives them a chance to grab their "share" of your earnings before you even see your paycheck. As we've said, under this system most Americans have become completely ignorant of how much they pay in income taxes. Not only that, they don't really know how much they actually earn by working! If you don't know how much you're paying in taxes, you're hardly going to complain about it.

Here's a nifty but depressing little experiment for you to try the next time April 15 rolls around. Approach some of your friends or coworkers and ask, "Say! Just curious, but how much income tax did you have to pay this year?" Admittedly, it's a pretty personal question. Don't be surprised if you end up getting a lot of "none of your business" responses. But among your friends and coworkers who do respond, listen closely and see how often you hear something like this in response: "I didn't have to pay anything. I'm getting some back."

Cringe.

Consider this response for a moment. These are the words of someone who may well have worked from sunup to sundown for fifty-two weeks in the previous year, with perhaps two weeks off for a vacation. Every two weeks or so, chances are, this person received a paycheck—with a substantial deduction for federal income taxes and payroll taxes. Then, the following April 15, you ask them how much tax they paid and what those deductions amounted to, and they have absolutely no clue. All they can tell you is how much their refund will be. Oh, happy day! They're getting some back! They're so thrilled with the refund of excess taxes seized by the government from their paychecks that they've missed the far more important fact: how much of their hard-earned wages the government actually keeps!

Think about it for a second: Can you see how easy this makes it for the government to seize and spend our money?

In one FairTax forum, a young lady said she wasn't interested in paying tax on everything she buys, because last year she didn't have to pay taxes at all. On April 15 she got a refund—five hundred whole dollars from the government! We then made her a sensational offer: If she'd let us take a thousand dollars out of her paycheck today, next year we'd promise to give her that thousand back—and she'd be twice as happy as she was with her five hundred bucks from the government!

She didn't get it. (Go figure.)

Let's take our polling of our friends and coworkers one step further. You don't have to wait until tax day to do this. This one works fifty-two weeks a year. Just ask a few people how much they make. That's all! Just "Hey, how much do you make a week?" Again, get ready for plenty of "none of your business" cold shoulders. But when you do get an answer, it's likely to be some figure preceded by the phrase "I take home . . ." For example, "I take home eight hundred and fifty bucks a week." Now, if you're an obnoxious talk show host (like some people we know), you may respond, "I didn't ask you how much you took home, I asked you how much you *made*."

Brook trout.[1]

A huge number of Americans, including both salaried and hourly workers, have no clear idea whatsoever of how much they actually earn during a particular pay period. They just know what's left after the federal government extracts

---

1. The authors give credit to former University of Georgia head football coach Ray Goff for the expression "brook trout." Imagine a blank stare and gaping mouth . . . slowly pulsating as the basic biological need for oxygen is satisfied.

the income taxes, the Social Security taxes, and the Medicare taxes. That money is gone—and the average worker doesn't even consider it part of his earnings in the first place. He's focused on what he "takes home."

Again, think about how wonderful that is for tax collectors. They seize the money, and it's not even missed.

This is a lesson that is not lost on other institutions in American life. Unions, for instance, know the value of getting their union dues taken from a worker's paycheck before the worker can get his hands on the money. This is what's known as a "union check-off," and it's often an integral part of union negotiations. Union members who actually have to write checks for their union dues are more apt to question the value they are receiving in return. Get the money before the worker receives his pay, and he'll never miss it—the same as our average taxpayer.

It wasn't always so. In the early years of the income tax, taxpayers would calculate the full amount of income taxes they owed for the previous tax year and write one check to the Internal Revenue Service. Your taxes were paid just as you pay your automobile insurance premium or your real estate property taxes today. You get your bill; you write your check. Before withholding came along, you can bet your life savings that people knew how much they were paying in income tax. You write the government a check for that kind of loot every year, and it has a way of sticking in the old memory bank.

That was a good thing for the individual taxpayer's sense of his fiscal well-being, at least. For politicians who want to raise taxes? Not so good.

Then came withholding.[2]

The popular story is that withholding was born of necessity during World War II because a reliable cash flow was needed to fund the war effort. Not so. Few people realize that withholding was a part of the first income tax law after the ratification of the Sixteenth Amendment. The 1913 law establishing the income tax allowed the federal government to withhold taxes from workers' paychecks just as it is done today. Then something happened that stopped the withholding juggernaut: The citizens of 1913, unlike our present-day variety, said "*nothing doing.*" They complained to their representatives in Washington, and in 1917 a law was passed barring the practice of withholding taxes. Taxpayers went back to paying their taxes in one lump sum, and politicians in Washington went back to their drawing boards.

But the politicians weren't ready to throw in the towel. They saw that withholding was the one way they could camouflage the actual tax burden pressed on the American people and further their political dream of spreading the scope and power of the federal government.

So when World War II came along, it provided the political class with the handy excuse they'd been seeking to put income tax withholding back on the table. War, after all, can be a great opportunity for politicians to manipulate the

---

2. For an excellent and comprehensive treatise on the origins of withholding see Charlotte Twight, Ph.D. (Economics), J.D., professor of Economics at Boise State University, "Evolution of Federal Income Tax Withholding: The Machinery of Institutional Change," *Cato Journal*, 14(3).

patriotic feelings of the American people. With the coming of the war, the funding needs of the federal government could no longer be covered by a tax on the wealthy; now it was time for everyone to chip in. What better way to garner public support than to tell all patriotic Americans that it was time to step up to the plate and fork over the cash. Instead of waiting for a year to pay your bill, Americans were to hand it over as they earned it. There was still substantial taxpayer opposition to withholding, but the politicians eventually won—even though they needed help from Donald Duck, among others, to pull off the victory.

The story of the political debate surrounding the implementation of tax withholding is a compelling lesson in the use of propaganda and outright dishonesty. While exhorting Americans to show their support for the war effort and our troops overseas by supporting an expansion of the scope of the income tax and tax withholding, politicians talked quite a different game behind closed doors and in the hearing rooms of Congress. In private, politicians shared their fears that taxpayers would simply refuse to pay if tax burdens increased by any appreciable amount.

The answer? Withholding.

Professor Charlotte Twight relates a very telling piece of testimony delivered by one particular U.S. Treasury official during hearings on the new withholding law. Transcripts of the hearing show the official made a reference to the "person against whom the [withholding] method was applied," and then quickly corrected himself to say "or I might say in whose *favor* it was applied." Official Washington clearly understood that withholding was to be a tool to be used *against* taxpayers, not a program to make their taxpaying experience more pleasant.[3]

And that was just the tip of the propaganda iceberg. Taxpayers were told of the many personal benefits they would derive from withholding. They wouldn't have to bother with funding savings accounts from which their taxes would be paid every year. Withholding would relieve them of that burden—not to mention the interest they would have earned on the money they were setting aside. Treasury Secretary Henry Morgenthau Jr. told Americans that they would find withholding to be a far more convenient way to pay their taxes. Convenience to the taxpayer was the official storyline—power to government was the reality.

Now we did mention Donald Duck a while back, didn't we? Where does this ill-tempered drake figure in this scenario? In 1942, at the urging of the Treasury Department, Walt Disney produced and distributed an animated feature called "The New Spirit." The cartoon was to be shown as a short subject in movie theaters across the nation . . . probably right after the newsreel featuring pictures from the battlefronts. So there was your pal and mine, Donald Duck, telling you that "it is your privilege to help your government by paying your tax and paying it promptly." Tens of millions of Americans saw this film, and Gallup reported that 37 percent

---

3. Charlotte Twight, Ph.D. (Economics), J.D., professor of Economics at Boise State University, "Evolution of Federal Income Tax Withholding: The Machinery of Institutional Change," *Cato Journal*, 14(3).

of the people felt that Donald Duck actually had a positive effect on their willingness to pay taxes.[4]

Thanks, Donald. We owe you one.

Evidently, though, propaganda and manipulation alone weren't quite enough to swing the public all the way over to the idea of tax withholding. Something else was needed . . . a big-time carrot.

In order to gain the necessary level of public support for income tax withholding, a fiction was created. It was called the Ruml Plan, cleverly named after the man who came up with the idea, one Beardsley Ruml. Here's the bill of goods the Ruml Plan helped sell to the American people. It seems very simple: if, starting in 1943, you allow us to start withholding taxes from your paychecks, then we'll forgive all of the taxes you owe for the year 1942 and you won't have to pay them when March 15 rolls around![5]

Before the promotion of the Ruml Plan, public support for withholding was shallow at best. After Americans became convinced that they'd be getting away with not paying taxes on one year's worth of income, though, the die was cast and support for withholding soared.

Now let's take a moment to apply some logic to this Ruml Plan. Were Americans really getting away with anything? Of

---

4. "Class Tax to Mass Tax: The Role of Propaganda in the Expansion of the Income Tax during World War II," *Buffalo Law Review,* 37(3).
5. Originally, Americans wrote the check to pay the income taxes due for their previous year on March 15 rather than April 15. Taxpayers with large balances due were also given the option of paying those taxes over the course of one year in four quarterly installments.

course not. Perhaps the best way to dispel any notion that this was a "tax elimination" scheme is to point out that the government's revenues wouldn't decline under the plan. Now, if you're going to forgive an entire year's income tax collections, you would expect government revenue to take quite a hit, wouldn't you? Well, it didn't. The simple truth was that, instead of paying the previous year's tax bill in one lump sum, wage earners would really be paying the previous year's taxes over the course of the current year, paycheck by paycheck, through the new withholding system. The politicians realized that expanding the income tax, while instituting the withholding scheme, would allow them to increase the government's tax revenues enough that it easily compensated for this supposed 1942 "tax forgiveness" offer.

There *was* one way the Ruml Plan could work for you: You could die. If you died at the beginning of 1943, your estate would owe no income taxes for 1942, and since your income would presumably stop with your death, you wouldn't experience the promised nirvana of withholding.

Oddly, arguments against the Ruml Plan were amazingly like arguments against tax cuts today. There was concern that the rich would benefit more than the poor from the plan to eliminate one year's worth of income tax revenues. Well, let's see: The more you earn, the more taxes you owed. The more you owed, the more you saved when those taxes were forgiven. What a concept! Some things never change.

The voters bought it, and with the able assistance of Donald Duck, Beardsley Ruml, and politicians looking for a way to raise taxes while softening the impact, the Current Tax

Payment Act of 1943 was finally signed into law.[6] The way was paved for accelerating the expansion of the federal government and collecting more taxes, all without any significant protests from the American people.

Let's focus for a moment on one date: April 15. Try to imagine April 15 without tax withholding. How would you feel as that dread day approached, knowing you were going to have to write a check to the IRS for many thousands of dollars? This would undoubtedly be the largest check most people wrote during the entire year.

Let's choose a nice even figure for your federal income tax liability for the previous year. We'll put it at $10,000. You've been fiscally prudent, putting some money into an investment account every month, knowing that this tax bill would come due. Finally, once April 15 rolls around, you sit down to write the check. At that moment, and probably for a considerable period of time thereafter, you'd be focused on the fact that you've just sent $10,000 of your savings, which you worked for and earned, to Washington to be spent on goodness-knows-what by politicians. Wouldn't you be pretty darn curious about just what the politicians were going to do with your money—and be fully ready to hold them accountable if you felt it was being squandered? Wouldn't the cost of

---

6. The final legislation calling for tax withholding actually contained only a 75 percent forgiveness of the previous year's taxes due. Provisions were also added to make sure that the wealthy were forced to pay income taxes on the so-called "windfall profits" they made from investments with companies engaged in the war effort.

government—that is, its cost to you—suddenly be at the very center of your thinking?

Contrast this to the reality of April 15 as we know it under the withholding scheme. Instead of being a day when Americans are focused on what the government is costing them, most of us are instead focused on how much we're getting back from that government! It's a day when we let the government know how big a check to write *us,* not a day the government takes a huge hunk out of our previous year's earnings. Now go back to that question we suggested you pose to your friends at the beginning of this chapter: "How much income tax did you have to pay this year?" See why your friends have no idea what the government is costing them each year? It's the magic of withholding, the answer to the free-spending politician's prayers.

Politicians know a good thing when they see it, and accordingly, since 1943, there have been plenty of efforts to expand the withholding scheme. In the 1970s, President Jimmy Carter attempted to have withholding extended to interest and dividends. This time Americans seemed to understand that having taxes withheld on their interest and dividend earnings before those taxes were actually due would cost them additional earnings. The effort failed, but it was revived a few years later in 1982. With the enthusiastic support of President Ronald Reagan, politicians cited the budget deficit as a reason to expand withholding to include dividends and interest earnings. Congress authorized the additional withholding measure in 1982 but, to put it mildly, the American people were not pleased. The withholding measure for interest and dividends was repealed a month after it went into effect. It makes you wonder: If withholding hadn't already been deeply entrenched in our system by the early 1980s, would Congress have been able to sneak it in under the noses of the American people?

There's a lesson here for proponents of the FairTax. Just as the political class underestimated the American people in the 1980s when we stopped government's blatant grab on our right to earn interest on our dollars, we can make the FairTax a reality if we band together today and exert unrelenting pressure on our politicians to bring it about. We made them withdraw their bid to withhold taxes on our interest—who's to say that history couldn't repeat itself with a surge of popular support for a repeal of the Sixteenth Amendment, the end of the income tax, and a transition to a consumption tax?

All across America, people are already asking: What will it take to make the FairTax a reality?

There's really only one answer, and that's *you*.

3

THE MYTH OF CORPORATE TAXES

In much the same way that we've targeted withholding for elimination, the FairTax also targets corporate taxes for elimination . . . and some people find this aspect of the Fair-Tax objectionable. These people might believe that corporations don't pay enough tax as it is, and they see no particular reason to lessen the burden. After all, haven't they been reading in the press about all of the obscene profits these corporations are making? The economic education of Americans is so woefully inadequate that many of us actually think we pay *less* as individuals when taxes are transferred to businesses and corporations.

I'll let you in on a closely guarded secret: those corporations aren't paying taxes now. When it comes right down to it, *no* corporation or business really pays taxes. The burden—all of it—falls on us.

There is only one entity in this country that actually pays taxes, and that entity is the individual. Businesses and corporations merely collect the taxes from individuals and pass them on to the government. Taxes are paid from wages, and in this country only individuals earn wages. It's even accurate to say that the assets of our federal government are owned by the people who live here and pay taxes—though exercising any degree of control over those assets might be difficult.

We believe that it's important for you to understand this concept: Businesses and corporations don't pay taxes, they merely collect taxes and pass them on. Exposing this fraud is central to encouraging you to become a rabid advocate of the FairTax.

So let's take this step by step.

First, we'll create a fictional corporation. We can give it a catchy name: FairTax Inc. Our company makes widgets—the best widgets money can buy. If you don't already have one of these widgets, you certainly want one. FairTax Inc. has one hundred shareholders. Its fifty employees make two hundred widgets every year, which the company sells for $100,000 each. (We told you these were good widgets, didn't we?) FairTax Inc.'s gross revenues equal $20 million a year. It costs the company about $18 million a year, including labor costs and all federal taxes, to produce and market those widgets. That leaves $2 million in profit.

Okay, now let's say that one day the federal government comes along with a 5 percent corporate tax increase. This means that FairTax Inc. will owe about $100,000 more in federal income taxes. (Don't pick nits with us here; we're simplifying the numbers to make a point.) So just where is the company going to get that extra hundred grand? Let's consider the possibilities:

1. It could pay the money out of the $2 million profit. Fine, that works! But to whom does that profit really belong? It belongs to the shareholders. You have one hundred shareholders sitting out there waiting for their dividend checks. Increase the taxes by $100,000 and each shareholder sees his dividend check decrease. See who's picking up the corporate tax now? The *shareholders,* not the *corporation.*

2. Raise the price of the widgets to cover the increased corporate tax, you say? Another great and time-tested idea—if you can raise the price without affecting your market share, that is. Pull that one off and you're one fine businessperson indeed. But who ends up paying the additional corporate income tax? That's right, you're catching on: The *customers* foot the bill, with the extra bucks they shell out for their favorite widget.

3. Well, maybe you can cut costs to cover the additional taxes. Fine, that's another solid solution. But just what costs are you going to cut? Maybe lay off a few employees and shoot for increased productivity? Good luck. At any rate, an individual—the fired employee—takes the hit. Cut back on employee benefits?

Again, the employees take the hit. Buy cheaper components to make your widgets? Yeah, that'll work, but the reason the Brand X components are cheaper is that they pay their employees less and offer limited benefits. Your original supplier takes a beating and passes it on to its employees and suppliers.

See where we're going? Just try finding one area where FairTax Inc. can cut costs without passing the impact on to some individual somewhere.

It's plain as the nose on George Washington's face: Only individuals create wealth. Only individuals retain wealth. Only individuals can have their wealth seized by the government in the form of taxes. Sure, the money may sift through corporate hands on the way to the U.S. Treasury, but the corporations only serve the role of collection agents and remitters. The bottom line: You pay the price.

If it's true that individuals are really shouldering the entire tax load, you're probably wondering: Why even go through the process of having corporate taxes in the first place? It's a good question, with a one-word answer: *deception.*

Tax collectors discovered long ago how convenient it was to disguise a significant percentage of government revenues as corporate taxes. Politicians realized that the average American knows no more about corporate accounting and taxation than Dan Marino does about hockey goaltending. After all, they run the schools, remember? Politicians can pledge to raise corporate taxes, and the myrmidons[1] will actually praise

---

1. Look it up. It's a great word. We all know a few. Maybe a lot.

them for it. It's a wonderful world indeed when you can look a citizen in the eye and say, "Hey, Pal, I'm going to take even more money out of your pocket by increasing corporate taxes," and the citizen shouts back, "Thank you very much, Senator! You da man!"

These politicians know that if they had to take all of the money they collect from the people in the form of corporate and business income taxes, and add it to the personal income taxes paid by individuals, they'd soon be peeking out of their office curtains at crowds of irate taxpayers armed with pitchforks. The ruse of the corporate income tax affords protection to the free-spending politician.

That said, taxes are a fact of corporate life. And, as you will read later, corporate managers and business owners spend an inordinate amount of time making business decisions based on tax consequences. This is because taxes are a major component of the cost of doing business—a cost that's reflected in prices.[2]

The burden on American corporations is huge, and we need to understand the magnitude of the problem—since, as we noted earlier, you and I are paying every penny of that burden when we buy corporate-produced goods at the checkout counter.

The corporate tax rate in the United States is the third highest in the industrial world, and the burden falls most heavily on small businesses. According to the Tax Foundation,

---

2. We're speaking here of the embedded taxes that are present in virtually every retail item we buy. More on this later.

just the time and effort of complying with our massively complex tax code costs the average small business about $724 for every $100 it pays in income taxes to the government.[3] It's hard to imagine a more incredible waste of human and business effort. In total, the director of the Congressional Budget Office believes that it costs American businesses somewhere between $400 and $500 billion—that's with a "B," my friends—just to comply with the complicated tax code. Five hundred billion dollars a year, with every single penny of it coming out of the pocket of some individual somewhere—either an owner, employee, shareholder, or customer—it's all there, hidden in the price you pay for every consumer item or service.

There's one more aspect of corporate taxation we need to bring up: lobbyists. Washington is crawling with a virtual army of high-income attorneys and accountants who earn their living doing one thing: manipulating and gaming the federal tax system for the benefit of their corporate clients. One goal of the FairTax proposal is to eliminate all business and corporate income taxes. As the FairTax movement gains more and more public support, the screams of alarm from this army of lawyers and accountants will be something to behold. After all, our plan will place their million-dollar incomes in dire jeopardy. They will fight back, hard and dirty, and it will be a no-holds-barred donnybrook. These lobbyists and lawyers aren't concerned with economic growth or the creation of jobs. Their one goal is to

---

3. As reported in "The Costs of Compliance," *Investor's Business Daily*, May 1, 1996.

preserve our horribly complicated and convoluted tax code—the code that sets the stage for their Beltway heroics and huge paychecks.

The money paid to the Washington lobbyists for tax code manipulation is just a small part of the total cost of complying with our tax laws. Money spent complying with the tax code is money that is not spent growing our economy and creating new jobs.

So how much does that come to? Next chapter.

4

OUR CURRENT TAX CODE: THE COST OF COMPLIANCE

We might hope to see the finances of the Union as clear and intelligible as a merchant's books, so that every member of Congress and every man of any mind in the Union should be able to comprehend them, to investigate abuses, and consequently to control them. Our predecessors have endeavored by intricacies of system and shuffling the investigation over from one office to another, to cover everything from detection. I hope we shall go in the contrary direction, and that, by our honest and judicious reformation, we may be able . . . to bring things back to that simple and intelligible system on which they should have been organized at first.

—Thomas Jefferson to Albert Gallatin, 1802

You might think that the bottom line on your individual or business tax return—the one that shows the total taxes you owe—pretty much tells the entire story of how much our tax system costs you every year. Well, you would be wrong—very wrong. The cost of our current system of taxation goes far beyond the actual taxes remitted to the U.S. Treasury. One of the beauties of the FairTax, as we'll see, is how little individuals and businesses have to pay just to comply with the law!

Think for a moment of the trouble you go through every year trying to get your annual tax return ready. In 2005 the estimated time the average American spent on the process was up to twenty-seven hours—that's more than a full day for the average taxpayer just to fill out his or her tax forms. Now don't you just love those hours you spend every year sitting cross-legged on the living room floor with bank statements, receipts, check stubs, and various other documents scattered around the room?

Then again, maybe you're one of the ever-growing number of Americans who just pass this responsibility off to an accountant or other tax preparer. In which case, we'll just restate the question: Don't you just love the money you spend every year paying someone to help you pay the government?

For some, the process of lining up receipts, looking for deductions, and poring over tax forms is so cumbersome, so infuriating, that they just throw in the towel every year and go the easy route: They take that stack of receipts and financial documents they've been collecting in that box under the bed for the past year and just send it down the garbage chute. These taxpayers have decided that the cost of claiming the tax deductions that are rightfully theirs is just not worth it. They throw their hands up and file a tax return with no deductions—thereby sending millions of hard-earned dollars, *which they don't really owe,* to the federal government. This is money that would stay in the taxpayer's pocket if the trouble and cost of complying with the tax code weren't so high. The numbers on this problem alone are astonishing. Would you believe that many taxpayers who *could* claim the coveted home mortgage interest deduction *decide not to* . . . just because they'd rather save an hour or two by opting for the short form instead?

This is yet another cost of compliance: the money the government keeps that otherwise would be refunded to the taxpayers.

Maybe you're one of those who have too much to lose, so you just suck it up, bear with the complexities of our tax code, and complete their horribly complicated returns. You view this as an unpleasant job that has just become a part of your yearly financial cycle, and you do it year after year, without ever giving any real consideration to how much it's costing you.

If we're going to win you over as a true fan of the FairTax, you need to have some idea of what the current tax code is costing you each and every year. The numbers are staggering, but you don't have to crunch them yourself. Others have already done it for you. In this chapter, you'll learn just how much our current income tax is costing individual taxpayers, corporate taxpayers, and the American economy year after year.

First, a question: What if your local bank sent you a notice telling you that it was going to start charging you $33 for every $100 that you deposit, just to cover the bank's cost of complying with banking regulations? Would you keep making deposits there? Of course not. You'd be better off keeping the money under your mattress, rather than giving up a full third of your money. Why then, are we all so willing to tolerate a tax system in which the government takes the first 33 cents out of every dollar we earn,[1] and then, in effect, charges us more just to comply with the law? Why in the world should it cost you so much money just to allow the government to seize the first 33 percent of each of your paychecks?

As we said, that bottom line on your tax return is just part of the story. There are other costs. Some of the costs are obvious, such as the time and money you spend on record-keeping and accountants just so you can end up with an accurate tax return every year instead of one that violates our impossible-to-understand tax laws.

But wait—you're not through yet! You've just begun. Have you ever stopped to calculate just how much money you lose each year because you have to make financial and business decisions aimed at reducing your tax obligation? Wouldn't it be better to make decisions designed to *maximize income,* rather than minimize taxes? For that matter, wouldn't you love it if the government allowed you to keep your money

---

1. Most Americans' paychecks are debited 25 percent for income taxes and nearly 8 percent for payroll taxes before the paycheck even reaches the hand of the worker. This, of course, doesn't even include the nearly 8 percent that every employer must pay on behalf of every employee . . . and virtually all economists agree that this extra 8 percent effectively comes right out of the employee's paycheck, too.

in an investment account of some kind, earning interest for *you,* until *you* decide to pay taxes to the federal government?

Well, that's how it would be with the FairTax.

Now, let's apply some real dollars to your tax compliance costs.

For several years, the Tax Foundation has calculated the costs of complying with the increasingly complicated federal tax code. They estimate that in 2002 individuals, businesses, and nonprofits spent 5.8 billion hours complying with the tax code—an effort that cost an estimated $194 billion.[2] Think about that number for a minute: 5.8 billion hours. If the average life expectancy is seventy-six years, then the 5.8 billion hours it takes to comply with our tax code in just one year would equal the combined lifespan of 8,700 Americans. It's as if we're throwing away the lives of 8,700 Americans every year, just to make sure we've all complied with the tax code. What an incredible waste of human potential and productivity.

Here's another way to look at it: What kind of a workforce would it take to cover those 5.8 billion hours? If you figure a standard workweek—eight hours a day, five days a week, a few weeks every year off for vacation—it adds up to a workforce of more than 2.77 million people. That's more people than work in the auto industry, the computer manufacturing industry,

---

2. Since this book was authored, the Tax Foundation has released a new report. This December 2005 report calculates that 6 billion hours and $265 billion were spent to comply with the federal income tax in 2005. We believe the point is made quite well using even the older 5.8 billion hour estimate. Source: Tax Foundation Special Report, "The Rising Cost of Complying with the Federal Income Tax," December 2005, No. 138 (www.taxfoundation.org).

the aircraft manufacturing industry, talk radio, and the steel industry in the United States *combined*. This is, by any measure, a huge and tragic waste of our human resources . . . and all of that to simply comply with the tax code.

Oh, and one more thing: Don't forget the roughly 100,000 people who work for the IRS, chewing up a budget of more than $10 billon a year. Don't worry, they'll find other things to do when the FairTax rolls in.

Now, some of you may be thinking: Is this really such a big deal? After all, isn't most of this cost paid by businesses? Isn't this just another cost of doing business?

Once again, the Tax Foundation is here to set us straight with the facts. Almost 56 percent of tax compliance costs are paid by businesses. Another 2.5 percent are paid by the nation's nonprofit organizations. That leaves almost 42 percent paid for by . . . guess who? That would be you. And the same principle we talked about earlier still holds: Whatever portion of the tax compliance costs businesses do pay, those costs will eventually be passed on to individuals—be they employees, customers, or shareholders. Except for churches and nonprofits, all wealth is held by individuals, and individuals end up paying the tab.

We don't want to get carried away with too many details here, but it's important that you have as complete an understanding of tax compliance costs as possible, without turning you into a gaggle of boring accountants. Our current tax structure constitutes a tremendous drag on our economy and on American productivity. You pay a good portion of the price for that inefficiency. So, we're going to hammer the point home just a bit more.

The costs of complying with the tax system take several forms. The Tax Foundation has categorized three separate types of tax compliance costs:

1. Wealthy individuals will spend tens of billions of dollars a year in tax planning. Among these "wealthy individuals" would be many people—your neighbor, for instance—who may not live a life of wealth and glamour, but who have holdings they'd like to protect from taxation. It's not unusual for a farmer, for instance, to spend tens of thousands of dollars each year with tax planners so that his heirs will be able keep the property safe from the death tax and continue to farm after he dies.
2. Both individuals and businesses spend countless dollars each year on tax seminars and educational forums, tax record keeping, and the preparation and filing of forms and returns.
3. Tax audits and litigation over tax returns are a deadly drain on the economy as a whole.

Of these three types of tax compliance costs, only the second is included in the Tax Foundation's $194 billion tax compliance cost estimate.

Now, let's hit a few more tax compliance costs—some you may not have thought about.

Have you ever heard of the concept of "opportunity costs"? An opportunity cost is money lost as a result of business decisions that prevented you from exploiting certain opportunities. Businesses and individuals with high incomes are familiar with these opportunity costs. In another page or two you will be also.

It will not surprise you to learn that businesses and high-income individuals routinely calculate the tax implications of a business decision. Some have estimated that nearly 80 percent of all business decisions at the highest corporate levels are made only after due consideration of the tax consequences involved. This, in and of itself, constitutes a tremendous drag on dynamic business decision making, and thus our economy.

You're not exempt. You have opportunity costs as well. In 2002, the government collected about $950 billion in individual income taxes. Most of this money was withheld from workers' paychecks and forwarded to the IRS every other week. But what if you had the opportunity to take that money—money you know you'll one day have to pay to the IRS—and invest it until your taxes are actually due? For example, if in 2002 taxpayers had been allowed to keep their money until it was due—and if they had invested that money in completely safe and secure T-bills—tax-paying Americans would have pocketed nearly *$24 billion* in interest payments. That's an opportunity cost. That is the cost taxpayers bear—the money taxpayers lose—because of the lost opportunity to invest their tax payments before they actually come due.

You're not yawning already, are you? Yeah, this may be a bit dull, but it's important. So suffer just a bit longer. The cost you pay for our current tax system isn't just reflected in the amount withheld from your paycheck. It goes much further than that. The opportunity costs of our tax system really began their steady increase in 1954. It was then that the income tax was placed at the center of our tax system. Since

1954, the number of words in our tax code has increased by nearly 500 percent. And that's just the increase in the *code*. It's the actual IRS regulations that tell you how to calculate, report, and pay your taxes. The number of words in the IRS *regulations* has increased by *939 percent*.

The more our tax code grows, the more complicated it becomes. The more complicated, the more it costs to comply and the greater the cost to you. Virtually every time our

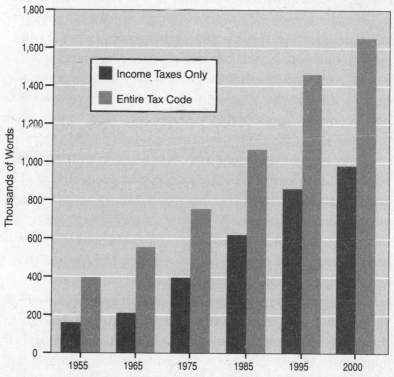

Source: The Cost of Compliance by Scott Moody, Senior Economist, Tax Foundation, February 2002.

FIGURE 4.1 Growth of the Tax Code: 1955–2000.

politicians and regulators have added to the verbiage of the IRS code and regulations, you have been told that their purpose was to make it easier for you. Politicians call it "tax reform" or "tax simplification." Nice try, but not true. In most cases, these added complexities are the result of some politician's desire to please a particular constituency . . . and usually at your expense.

Indeed the tax cuts of 1997, and the cuts and code changes that followed, have combined to make the code so much more complex that a greater percentage of taxpayers are now forced to consult professional tax experts to help prepare their returns than at any point in history.

Taxpayers spend all of this money on tax return preparation . . . and to what end? In most cases, it's to create, sign, and submit a tax return that's simply incorrect!

The FairTax Plan, on the other hand, is simple to understand and simple to comply with. It is black and white. If you present ten accountants with a FairTax problem, you'll get the same answer from each and every one. Not so with our present system. Some years ago, *Money* magazine sent the exact same economic data for a family's tax calculation to forty-nine separate professional tax experts. Of the forty-nine returns they received, no two were alike . . . and not one of them was correct. You can't expect much better results when you call the IRS for help—that is, if you can get through to them in the first place. Repeated studies have shown that if you call the IRS help line to get help in preparing your return, the answer you get will be wrong more than half of the time.

As discussed earlier, the Tax Foundation estimates of compliance costs cover only those costs incurred responding to the IRS. Earlier in this chapter, we recited Tax Foundation figures showing the number of man-hours and the total cost for individual compliance costs at $194 billion. In 2005, the last year for which statistics were available, the Tax Foundation estimated that cost at $265 billion. Add to that the time and money spent by businesses and investors calculating the tax implications of their business decisions, and you can figure at least half again as much. According to the current director of the Congressional Budget Office, making "tax decisions" rather than "economic decisions" (that is, making decisions that will reduce your taxes rather than increase your income) is a practice that costs our economy 18 percent of our gross domestic product[3]—a whopping $2 trillion loss in the GDP.

Adding up all these costs, it's a safe guess that somewhere in the neighborhood of $500 billion a year is spent to comply with the code. That's a $500 billion blow to our economy, all of it spent just to collect no more than three times that amount in tax revenue. This isn't $500 billion that makes its way into government spending programs, it's $500 billion in compliance costs and lost opportunities.

This is not inefficiency. This is stupidity!

What would be different under the FairTax Plan? Well, try to imagine what it would be like for a business owner or a corporate board of directors to contemplate a business expansion or other business move without having to give a second thought to the tax implications—because there wouldn't

---

3. The single economic figure that represents the total productivity of America.

be any tax implications. The decision would be based solely on what's good for the business, the employees, and the stockholders, not on how such a move might possibly violate some obscure section of the tax code or IRS regulations. This freedom to be a business owner and not a tax planner will, in and of itself, lead to unprecedented growth and expansion opportunities for American businesses.

And as for you, the individual? Your tax compliance costs drop to absolutely nothing. Zero. Zip. Nada. You earn your money and put it to work for you, not for the federal government. And there that money stays, working for you and earning for you, until the time that you elect to use that money for a purchase at the retail level. Then, and only then, do you pay a tax. No complicated decisions, no tedious bookkeeping, no saved receipts and tax reporting forms. Oh, and no audits. No fire-breathing IRS agents threatening the financial security of you and your family. If you buy something, you pay taxes. If you work, save, or invest, you don't.

And April 15? It becomes just another lovely spring day.

5

THE EMBEDDED COSTS OF OUR TAX CODE

Until now, there has never really been any compelling reason for you to ponder the question of just how much of the money you pay for a consumer item actually ends up in federal government coffers. You pay for your loaf of bread, and you take it home. You eat it, or you throw it out when that green fuzzy stuff starts growing on it. Simple as that.

Well, it's just not as simple as that—though it could be. Now that we've looked at hidden withholding, hidden corporate taxes, and hidden compliance costs, we can start to understand how all of those costs end up coming out of our pockets.

Whenever you buy any consumer item—a loaf of bread, a can of dog food, a car, a house, or a bowl of chili—part of the cost goes to the people who had a hand in producing and selling you that item, and part of the cost is given to the federal government as taxes.

We'll use a loaf of bread as our example here—after all, pretty much everyone buys bread—though any other consumer item or service would do. There are a lot of people who are involved in getting that loaf of bread to your table, and every one of them has a tax liability attached to his or her particular place in the bread and economic food chain. When you buy that loaf of bread, you're paying a portion of all of the bills, including tax bills, of every person or business entity that had anything to do with that bread, from before the wheat was planted up until the loaf of bread ends up in that plastic bag in the back seat of your minivan.

Here's just a partial list: First comes the seed producer, followed by the farmer who buys the seed to plant wheat. The seed producer is a taxpayer, and those taxes are reflected in the price he charges for seed. The farmer also buys things like fertilizer, irrigation equipment, fuel for his tractors, and labor. All bought from tax-paying businesspeople. You also have the trucking company that gets the raw materials to the processors. The processors are in this to make money, as are the bakery, the food distributor, and the grocery store. Taxpayers all. Then there's the company that made the packaging materials for your bread, and the farmer who grew the little sesame seeds you see on the crust. And don't forget the company that makes that little plastic gizmo that's supposed to reseal the bag—you know, the little plastic thing that we all throw away the first time we grab a slice. Whoever made that plastic thingie pays taxes . . . and passes the cost off to the bakery . . . which passes the cost off to you.

Does that seem like enough? Don't forget the thousands of companies it takes to manufacture the trucks, tractors, and plows, and to explore, recover, ship, and refine the oil that becomes gasoline to fuel these machines. Then you have marketing companies, advertising agencies . . . not to mention the talk show host who makes the big bucks with a personal endorsement for the bread company. The list almost never ends, and every single entity on that list is paying taxes. That means when you buy that loaf of bread you're paying a portion of those taxes all the way down the line.

Wait! We almost forgot. If we're really going to be thorough here, let's not forget rent, travel, health care, utilities, labor, and on and on. Every one of those entities has income taxes and payroll taxes and accountants and attorneys to avoid the taxes. Okay, so not all of these costs fall into the tax category—but some do. We bring them up to demonstrate that all of these elements make up a part of the cost of the consumer goods we buy from these corporations and individuals, and they're all eventually paid by the end consumer. We call these costs embedded taxes.

Okay . . . so what's the tab? When you bought that loaf of bread, just how much of the price represented the total combined tax costs of every person or business entity that worked to put that loaf on the grocery store shelf?

An extensive study of tax costs was completed a few years ago by Dr. Dale Jorgenson, then chairman of the Harvard Economics Department. On average, Jorgenson concluded, 22 percent of the price paid for a consumer product represents embedded taxes. That means that for every dollar you spend on a loaf of bread, twenty-two cents ends up being passed on to the government somewhere along the line in the form of taxes.

Now, to further your education on embedded taxes, here's a chart prepared by Jorgenson that shows just how much prices for certain consumer goods might be expected to decrease once the embedded taxes are removed!

As you can see from the chart, embedded taxes—and the consequent price reductions after those taxes are removed— vary from about 15 percent for leather goods to about 26 percent for services, including government services. However,

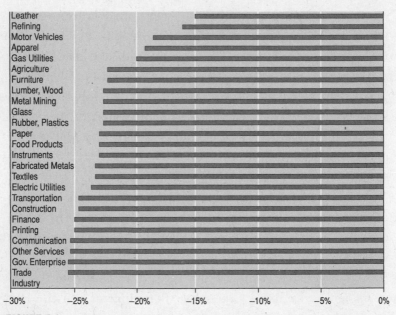

FIGURE 5.1 Prices Deline without Embedded Costs of the Tax Code: Percent Change in Prices.

on average, 22 percent of what you spend is supporting the government.[1]

That last thought bears some amplification. Look at it this way. When you get your paycheck, the federal government has already taken its pound of flesh for income taxes, Social Security taxes, and Medicare taxes. If you think you're through paying taxes to the federal government at that point, you're sadly mistaken. As you've just seen, every single time you spend a dollar at the retail level on virtually any consumer product or service, you're paying another hefty chunk to the Beltway crowd. You're not through paying taxes until the bread is buttered and on your plate! And if you decide you want toast . . . well, just consider the tax burden paid by the utility industry that's firing up that toaster for you. You'll pay your share of that, too!

Elsewhere in this book we discuss the amazing sums of money that individuals and corporations spend trying to reduce their tax burden. Yes, those costs too are passed on

---

1. Jorgenson's embedded cost estimate requires some further explanation. His calculation includes the elimination of federal, state, and local taxes because he—as do we—assumes that state and local governments will follow the federal government and abolish income taxes. However, his estimates presented here are simply what he expects to happen in year one of a consumption tax. Over time, of course, even more taxes will be driven from the price, and prices will drop an average of 29 percent according to the Jorgenson report. As federal receipts to be replaced dwarf state and local receipts to be replaced, we conservatively use 22 percent to estimate the long-term embedded costs of federal taxes alone.

down to the end consumer . . . you. It's all part of the embedded cost of our current tax code.

We've mentioned that these embedded costs exist not only in consumer goods, but in services as well. Another example might help.

When you go to your doctor for a routine visit, you're probably aware that the fee you and your insurance company pay covers the doctor's overhead and income. But what are the elements of this overhead? Have you thought about how much your doctor pays into the payroll tax system to augment his or her employees' Social Security and Medicare taxes? And what about all the embedded taxes your doctor paid when purchasing all of that sophisticated equipment, not to mention the endless monthly outlay for cotton swabs and tongue depressors? Depressing, isn't it? Add to that the thousands of dollars (or tens of thousands of dollars) spent each year on accountants, attorneys, and insurance salespeople to protect against malpractice? You pay for that, too—every penny. Taxes roll downhill, too . . . not just that other stuff.

Now, just why is it so important that you understand how much federal tax income is embedded in the goods and services you purchase? Because one of the beauties of the FairTax is that the price of American consumer goods and services relative to your take-home pay will decline by roughly the same amount as the proposed FairTax rate of 23 percent. This very nearly makes everything a wash.

Consumer prices will go down? you say. *How can you be sure?*

One of the most frequent concerns we hear about the FairTax Plan is whether consumer prices will actually go down once all these embedded taxes are removed. Economists and policy experts who have studied the FairTax proposal are unanimous in their agreement that the cost of consumer goods and services will indeed fall, but our experience is that the general public needs a bit of convincing.

You've already learned of the extensive studies showing that the level of embedded federal taxes in the goods and services we purchase averages around 22 percent. If these embedded taxes were to disappear—that is, if the tax burdens of all the corporations, businesses, and individuals involved in the manufacture, marketing, and sale of these items were to be removed—these businesses would experience an immediate increase in their profit margins that would roughly equal that 22 percent. Why, people want to know, wouldn't these businesses just keep that extra 22 percent and take a big ride on the windfall profit gravy train?

Why indeed?

Well . . . let us ask you this question. Why not just raise your prices about 22 percent and take advantage of that extra profit anyway? The answer is clear. If one business suddenly raises its prices by 22 percent, other competing businesses are going to seize their opportunity to underprice the competition—and eat them for lunch. It's a simple matter of marketplace competitiveness.

Okay . . . so let's set up a bunch of competing companies in one particular product group—say, America's T-shirt makers. Let's say that T-shirts cost about eight dollars a piece to make, and sell for ten bucks. Americans seem to *need* T-shirts with fun little slogans, so the price competition is intense. Now, what happens once the FairTax Bill passes and is signed into law? Suddenly the cost to the retailer for the T-shirt drops by $1.76. This means he's purchasing T-shirts for $6.24 instead of $8.00, and selling them for $10.00 a shot. The retailer is now making $3.76 per T-shirt instead of $2.00. That's an increase of $1.76 in the retailer's profit. But wait! We're not through yet. The retailer is also off the hook for business and corporate income taxes and payroll taxes. This means that instead of profitting $2.00 per shirt and then paying taxes, the retailer now makes $3.76 that is all tax free.

So here you have the T-shirt sellers eyeing each other. They've all experienced a quick and dramatic increase in their profits. Life is good. Then one T-shirt retailer decides to try to grab a larger market share by lowering prices. The other T-shirt retailers aren't going to let him get away with that, so they follow suit. In the meantime, the various companies who supply goods and services to the T-shirt manufacturers are also trying to grab bigger market shares by dropping their prices. Everywhere you look, companies in every stage of the manufacturing, marketing, and retail food chain are dropping prices, trying to increase their competitive advantage. Soon, very soon, these competitive market pressures force prices down to a level where corporate profit margins are pretty much where they were before the passage of the FairTax.

And you? Your retail price for T-shirts has dropped to around $7.80 each. That's $2.20 less than you were paying. When you add the FairTax to the price of your T-shirt, you're right up there within pennies of where you were.

We actually have a real-life scenario to present to you that illustrates how quickly prices will fall once the embedded taxes are removed. We take you to December 31, 1995. The U.S. Congress was engaged in some budget disagreements that caused an expiration of the federal airline ticket tax. At first, all the airlines tried to hold ticket prices steady. The expiration of the airline tax made for extra profits in those prices—money the airlines needed desperately. In just a matter of days, the wall started to crumble. All it took was one small airline trying to create a competitive advantage by lowering ticket prices. One by one the other airlines followed, and in short order the tax cut went into the consumers' pockets, not the airlines'. And what happened when the airline ticket tax was reinstated? The prices went right back up. There's your real-life proof of our theory: If the pressure to reduce prices will compel an industry that's struggling to survive to lower ticket prices, then there's no doubt the same pressures will work with businesses that already have a healthy profit margin.

If you're looking for scholarly support for the proposition that prices will fall once the embedded taxes are removed, we can check back with Dr. Dale Jorgenson's "The Economic Impact of the National Retail Sales Tax."[2] "Since producers would no longer pay taxes on profits or other forms of capital income under the NRST [national retail sales tax] and workers would no longer pay taxes on wages," Jorgensen writes, "prices received by producers . . . would fall by an average of 20 percent." The result? "In the long run producers' prices . . . would fall by almost 30 percent under the NRST."

---

2. Final Report to Americans for Fair Taxation, May 18, 1997.

By this point, you should be able to do the math yourself. Once the FairTax takes effect, you will be in complete control of your paycheck as nothing will be withheld—and your purchasing power for t-shirts and all other goods and services will be almost exactly what it was before the FairTax.

But there's something more: Under the FairTax Plan, you'll also be receiving a check every month from the federal government equal to the amount of sales tax you would spend on the basic necessities of life for that month.

Yup, you heard that right: The government will be covering your tax burden for the basic necessities of life in the form of a regular check in your mailbox.

How would that work? Read on.

6

BRINGING AMERICAN BUSINESS BACK HOME

There's one more point we need to make before we get into the details of the FairTax Plan. We've already described the incredibly high costs individual and corporate taxpayers suffer just to comply with our Internal Revenue Code. We've also detailed the 22 percent embedded taxes that exist in virtually all consumer goods and services.

The effect of these hidden taxes on the American consumer is only part of the story. There's yet another great cost to our economy resulting from the federal income tax and its onerous regulations . . . and this cost is paid by the American worker, in the form of American jobs and businesses lost to more friendly tax structures and havens overseas.

Politicians and pundits create quite a bit of controversy over American corporations moving their headquarters abroad. These businesses have been called everything from "corporate Benedict Arnolds" to un-American tax cheats. These corporations aren't moving headquarters overseas because they relish the challenge of learning new languages. They're moving for one simple reason: to escape a punishing tax structure here at home.

This is an easy issue for a politician to demagogue. Painting a picture of some greedy board of directors sitting in an oak-paneled conference room somewhere making a decision to move the corporate headquarters to Bermuda, Europe, or the Caribbean is an easy way to outrage the average American. Yet the truth is that—under our current tax structure—the corporate boards that make these decisions are acting in the best interests of their shareholders, employees, and customers.

As soon as the FairTax Plan becomes law, these overseas corporate offices will be filled with packing boxes, and the phone lines of real estate agents all over America will be buzzing with the sound of expatriate corporations looking to return to their homeland.

Though you may not realize it, the United States treats its corporate citizens in a completely different manner from most other industrialized countries. We'll illustrate this with a simple comparison of an American-based automaker (we'll call it Americar) to an automaker based in France (Francocar).

At the end of every tax year, after all the year's cars have been sold and the earnings are totaled, Americar will pay

corporate income taxes in the United States for earnings realized in the United States, just as Francocar will pay taxes in
France for earnings realized in France. The similarity ends
there. If Americar sets up a sales and distribution operation
in France, it has to pay corporate income taxes to the United
States on earnings realized in France. If Americar does happen to incur any French corporate income tax liability, our
laws may allow a credit for those taxes to be applied to the
taxes due the U.S. government—but the difference will be
sent to Washington, D.C.

Francocar gets much more favorable treatment from its
government. If Francocar creates a division to sell cars in the
United States, it will only owe taxes to the U.S. government
for earnings realized from that operation. Francocar, on the
other hand, will owe no taxes to the French government for
earnings realized overseas.

When the corporate income tax disappears with the passage of the FairTax, this disparity will disappear, and this
particular incentive to move American corporations offshore
will have been eliminated.

Let's consider these tax implications with another
example. This time we'll use actual automobiles—the
Cadillac from General Motors and the venerable Mercedes-
Benz. General Motors makes its Cadillac luxury cars and
sells them at home and around the world. When a new
Cadillac rolls off the assembly line to an automobile dealer
in Nebraska, that embedded tax rolls right along with
it. Now, consider the Mercedes-Benz. The Mercedes is manufactured in Germany, where the largest tax component
is the notorious value-added tax (VAT). The VAT differs

substantially from the FairTax in that the VAT is a tax on the increase in value of any product at each stage in its production cycle. When a new Mercedes is exported from Germany to Nebraska, to compete head-to-head there with a new domestically produced Cadillac, the German government refunds the VAT to Mercedes. The Mercedes, then, comes to America with a minimal tax component in its price, to compete here with the Cadillac carrying the embedded tax. Does that sound like a fair fight to you? The Mercedes has a tax-driven competitive advantage, so it looks like you'll be driving around with a star on your hood for a few years. Things aren't any better when the Cadillac is exported to Germany for sale. The embedded tax crosses the pond with the Cadillac, and for good measure the Germans add a VAT to the price of our Cadillac before it appears on a showroom floor. Again, competitive advantage to Mercedes.

Now, is there *anything* about this process that seems equitable to you? Are you starting to get a hint as to why American products are less competitive in our global marketplace?

So just how do our American manufacturers deal with these tax inequities? For one thing, they move their production facilities offshore to a nation that has a more export-friendly tax structure, such as the VAT. Then they move their corporate headquarters offshore to a nation with a more friendly tax treatment of capital and labor.

The first of those two alternatives has sent about four million jobs offshore. The second is why European/American mergers such as DaimlerChrysler end up with headquarters in Stuttgart and not Detroit or New York City.

If we were to pass the FairTax and eliminate all taxes on capital and labor, and tax personal consumption instead, we would be the only nation in the world whose companies could sell into a global economy with no tax component in the price system. (Most nations that rebate the VAT to their companies on export still have some income and payroll taxes in the price system.) Can you imagine what that would mean to corporate leaders around the world?

First, the only way for foreign competition to compete with our companies would be for them to build their next plant in the United States. That way, they too could build their products without having to account for that extra tax burden in their pricing, and they could use American workers—the most productive in the world. Second, the tax component would fall out of our goods and services, and the American worker would get an increase in purchasing power. Millions of new jobs would be created. And the new workers filling them—whether they came from within our borders or elsewhere—would be contributing to our retirement programs and our government treasury every time they bought a loaf of bread.

Earlier in this chapter, we mentioned Mercedes-Benz. The Mercedes automobile is built by DaimlerChrysler, a company born of a merger between Daimler-Benz and Chrysler Corporation. John Loffredo was the vice president and chief tax counsel for the new company. In May 1999, Loffredo testified before Congress about the tax consequences of that merger of automotive giants—and along the way offered his testimony as an encouragement to Congress to change our tax laws. "[T]he U.S. tax system puts global companies at a decisive disadvantage," Loffredo told Congress. "This issue became a major concern and when the time came to choose whether the new company should be a U.S. company or a foreign company, management chose a company organized under the laws of Germany."

Mr. Loffredo went on to testify that a hypothetical "ChryslerDaimler" headquartered in the United States would face a 67.5 percent tax rate, while the actual Daimler-Chrysler, headquartered in Germany, pays only 44 percent.

You see, then, that our current tax system punishes U.S. corporations who try to expand their businesses overseas—whereas foreign corporations enjoy a competitive advantage over American corporations because of the more favorable tax treatment they receive from their governments. With the implementation of the FairTax, the international corporate playing field changes drastically, and the advantage immediately shifts to America.

With the FairTax, there will no longer be *any* reason for American corporations to move their headquarters overseas. After all, what sense would it make to move a corporate headquarters abroad in order to avoid some corporate income taxes when corporations no longer *pay* corporate income taxes in America? Bermuda might not be happy with the consequences, but the corporate headquarters staff will be. They get to move back home, and Bermuda once again becomes a vacation destination rather than a workplace.

Let's not forget the impact of the FairTax on foreign corporations. You see, they don't like paying taxes any more than we do.

Whether you're building automobiles or widgets, mixing perfumes or creating clothing fashions, making shoes or kitchen appliances and cabinets, you're going to sit up and take notice of the fact that you can now do business in America with no tax on labor or capital. From manufacturing to real estate, the gold rush will be on as foreign businesses rush to expand their bottom line by locating facilities in the greatest tax haven the industrialized world has ever known . . . the United States. This, of course, means more jobs for Americans. More jobs equal higher wages. Higher wages equal more spending. More spending equals more sales tax revenues to the U.S. government.

Can anyone find a loser in this scenario? Well, perhaps some foreign governments might find themselves a bit irritated as they see businesses rushing to participate in the new American economy, but for now we'll file that in the folder marked "Their Problem." Back here in the good old U.S. of A., we'll just be content to watch these new business facilities open their doors as tens of thousands of Americans march through to their new jobs . . . earning incomes that aren't taxed.

7

THE BIRTH OF THE FAIRTAX

The idea of changing the way we fund the federal government is certainly not new. As we've already shown, the problems have been around for decades. And so has the idea of switching from a tax on income to a tax on consumption.

The genesis of the consumption tax plan that would become the FairTax occurred in Houston, Texas. A Houston businessman served on the boards of several major corporations. After returning from one board meeting, the businessman complained to friends that fully 80 percent of the meeting was essentially wasted on discussions of the tax implications of virtually every business decision they discussed. "We should be worrying about our customers, our employees, and our shareholders," the businessman complained, "not the federal government."

The businessman kept up his lamentations until one of his friends finally issued a challenge. "Well, why don't you do something about it?"

Thus began the group Americans for Fair Taxation (FairTax.org).

The call went out for donations, and in short order several million dollars were raised. FairTax.org began soliciting proposals from several major universities for research and studies on how to reform our tax system. At that point, no particular plan was favored. The flat tax, the VAT, consumption taxes—all were on the table. The goal of FairTax.org was to develop a system that would raise the same amount of revenue for the government as our current income tax system, but which would be less intrusive, abusive, coercive, and corrosive. Oh . . . and less frustrating as well.

Enlisting the help of economists at several major universities, FairTax.org commissioned a new body of research—including polls and focus groups—to see what the American people wanted. During these focus groups, participants would sit with a professional facilitator for hours just discussing taxes—the current system, alternative systems, possibilities, and impossibilities.

As the studies, research, polls, and focus groups continued, FairTax.org's attention was steadily focused on a system that would be far less difficult to understand and far more efficient at raising required revenues for the operation of the federal government—a method of taxation that would be totally voluntary, that would allow all citizens to pay what they choose, when they choose, by how they choose to spend their money. That system—a national sales tax on goods and services sold at the retail level—became known as the FairTax, a name suggested by one enthusiastic focus-group participant.

Today, FairTax.org is leading hundreds of thousands of volunteers to carry the banner of the FairTax. The group's heavily trafficked website is an encyclopedia of knowledge for anyone interested in exploring the details of the FairTax. There you can learn the latest news from the legislative front, sign a petition in favor of the FairTax, sign up for e-mailed updates, volunteer to work for passage of the FairTax, and contribute to the cause.

Whenever some politician, pundit, or organization uses false or misleading data to critique the FairTax, the keepers of the FairTax.org website are ready with a well-researched rebuttal.

With luck, someday they won't have to work so hard.

8

THE FAIRTAX
EXPLAINED

At last, we're through with the preliminaries. You've read a brief history of our present federal income tax. You have a basic understanding of how tax withholding came along. You understand that the amount withheld from your paychecks, and that extra check many of you have to write on April 15, is only part of the story. And you've seen how the prices of consumer goods have already been driven up by a 22 percent embedded tax—a tax that drives jobs offshore and strains the budgets of low- and middle-class families.

Now that you've read how the FairTax Plan was born in the first place, it's time to introduce you to the details of plan itself.

First . . . please notice that this is not a long and complicated chapter. Why? Because the FairTax concept is clear and easy to understand—the way a tax code should be. With the FairTax, every American will understand just what their tax obligation is, and know when they're paying it. The FairTax will replace tens of thousands of pages of IRS rules and regulations with a tax code so simple it could be inscribed on the back of the "Sorry you lost your job!" condolences cards you could be sending to the laid-off workers at your local IRS office.

For those of you who will be talking to your congressman and senators about this idea, the FairTax bill is numbered H.R. 25 in the U.S. House of Representatives and S.25 in the U.S. Senate. Its official title is the FairTax Act of 2005.

If you need to carry it around on a note card (and we recommend that), the FairTax can be explained as follows:

When passed and signed into law the FairTax will repeal:

- The individual income tax
- The alternative minimum tax (AMT)
- Corporate and business income taxes
- Capital gains taxes
- Social Security taxes
- Medicare taxes (along with all other federal payroll taxes)

- The self-employment tax
- Estate taxes
- Gift taxes

All of those lovely taxes will be replaced with a single-rate personal consumption tax—a simple sales tax—on new goods and services.

Now, before we go any further, let's cover two things that the FairTax *isn't*. The two points that follow are extremely important because there are far too many columnists and pundits who seem to have no real idea of what they're talking or writing about when dealing with the FairTax:

- The FairTax is not a VAT or value-added tax similar to European VATs. VATs are added at every stage of production and hide tax costs in the price of goods. In contrast, the FairTax is levied once and only once—at the retail cash register—and it is printed on the sales receipt for all to see.
- The FairTax is a *replacement for*—not an addition to— our current federal taxes. It's simply a new and equitable method for raising the same amount of money our old and complicated code does today. Don't let anybody fool you into thinking this is a tax increase . . . and don't any of you fool your friends into thinking that it's a tax cut. It is neither. It is simply a tax replacement.

Now, let's get into the details.

The FairTax Act abolishes all taxes on income. In place of the many taxes we pay today—the corporate income tax, personal income tax, Social Security and Medicare taxes, and all the others listed earlier—consumers will pay an embedded personal consumption tax in the amount of 23 percent[1] on all goods and services sold at the retail level. Note, please, that we said "retail level." The 23 percent tax will not be imposed on the sale of used or previously owned items. Your garage sales are safe.

The FairTax is revenue neutral. In other words, the sales tax rate will be set to ensure that the federal government—and all the programs within it, including Social Security and Medicare—will receive from the national retail sales tax exactly what they had been receiving under the current tax system. This isn't about cutting spending or changing government benefits. It's simply a plan to change the way Americans fund their federal government.

The FairTax will also provide for strong taxpayer rights. Taxpayers will no longer be compelled to carry the burden of proof of compliance on tax matters. Under the FairTax, the burden of proof in tax disputes will be on the federal government. Citizens will be entitled to a refund, by the government, of all professional fees paid in the course of a dispute with the government over the payment of taxes unless it is established that the taxpayer's position was substantially unjustified.

How will it work? The Treasury Department will contract with the states for the states to administer the pro-

---

1. The rate set forth in H.R. 25 is currently 23 percent. At this writing, economic studies are under way that could result in the tax rate's being somewhat lower.

gram. For the forty-five states that already have sales taxes, this will not be a significant additional burden. The federal government will pay the states one quarter of 1 percent of what they collect in exchange for their services in collecting the consumption taxes and passing them on to the federal government. The same amount will also be paid to the business that collects the tax and remits it to the state agency.

As already stated, the tax will be levied against *all* goods and services. Yes, you will pay a tax to your doctor. In fact, approximately 26 percent of the money you pay the doctor today represents the embedded cost of the tax system—so look for your doctor's fees to go *down* by as much as, if not more than, the amount of the consumption tax he will collect.

Why tax your medical care? We need to be clear about this. Government ought to be neutral; it shouldn't allow politicians to pick winners and losers. Doctors, dentists, lawyers, and accountants should not be treated any differently from their neighbors who happen to be retailers. If their neighbors collect the tax, they should, too.

The same argument, about government's being neutral, applies to Internet and catalog sales, too. Several recent laws have placed a moratorium on taxing the Internet. Those laws dealt with a tax on *accessing* the Internet, not charging a sales tax on things sold there. Sales taxes and use taxes apply to Internet sales today, but Internet shoppers simply fail to pay them. In the spirit of government marketplace neutrality, that should change. We fail to understand why the couple down the street who built a bookstore in our community, vote in our elections, go to our churches and synagogues, and hire our kids for the summer should be put at a 7 percent disadvantage to Amazon.com!

The FairTax would also treat government purchases as taxable purchases. State, local, and federal government purchases will pay the tax. This is somewhat controversial, so let's walk through the idea.

Governments, just like individuals, currently pay the 22 percent embedded tax cost in every item they purchase. Governments also pay the employer's share of the Social Security tax on each dollar earned by an employee, up to $94,200. Ditto for the Medicare tax on each dollar of employee earnings. Governments will save a considerable amount of money when all of these operational costs go away. The FairTax should not be a windfall for governments. They will realize the savings when the embedded taxes are removed; they then get to pay the consumption tax along with everyone else. Look at it this way: Where does each dollar the federal government spends paying the FairTax go? You got it: *Right back to the federal government.* Remember, the FairTax is neutral. It plays no favorites. We've had enough of this "playing tax favorites" game with the present system and the influence of the K Street lawyers and lobbyists.

Is there another reason to treat governments like everyone else under the FairTax? You bet. Governments have this nasty little propensity to engage in businesses that compete with the very taxpayers who fund the government and therefore pay the salaries of the government employees. What a deal! Go into business in competition with someone, and then make *them* pay *your* employees! State governments use prison labor to compete with taxpaying businesses. Prison industries in many states sell cleaning chemicals to other governments. Municipal governments sell gas and electricity. They want to play the game? Fine—they should pay the tax.

By requiring governments to pay a tax on their purchases, the FairTax eliminates the competitive advantage over private business that governments have today. This would cause governments to divest themselves of businesses, from the sale of electricity to the collection of garbage. This—we believe—is a good thing!

If there's one important thing to remember about the FairTax, though, it's that the plan all but eliminates the total tax burden on middle- and lower-income Americans, allowing them to save their money (instead of handing it off to the government) and judge for themselves when and how they're comfortable making taxable purchases.

Despite that fact, one of the most frequently aired concerns about the FairTax is whether it will pose an unfair burden on lower-income Americans. We can understand how, upon hearing the basic premise of the FairTax, some people might wonder, "How in the world can a poor person, who's already struggling to make ends meet, pay a 23 percent sales tax on top of everything else they have to pay?"

The answer is that the FairTax treats everybody fairly— lower-income Americans included—because it provides that the federal government will send every family in America a *prebate* (that is, an advance rebate) to cover taxes on the basic necessities of life. Every head of household will receive this prebate every single month, to reimburse every American family for the sales tax that family will pay on all spending up to the federal poverty level, plus a few dollars thrown in to prevent any marriage penalty. The result? Low-income families, and many middle-income families, would be exempted from paying the national retail sales tax on all or most of their spending.

How will this work? Read on.

9

THE FAIRTAX PREBATE: THE KEY TO FAIRNESS

Perhaps you noticed that, in quite a few congressional races around the country last year, some candidates tried to frighten voters into believing that their opponent, a supporter of the FairTax, was planning to burden them with a horrible new tax. Here's how they spun it: Their opponent was going to *add* a 23 percent federal retail sales tax on everything we buy—implying, if not claiming outright, that this would be in addition to all the other taxes we're already paying!

Is this effective politics? Oh, yeah, you bet it's effective! Can you imagine how frightened any American—let alone one from the middle- or lower-income levels—would be at the prospect of paying another 23 cents out of every dollar that they spent? Anyone who believed that a candidate was going to do such a thing should not only have voted against that candidate, they should feel compelled to get out there and raise money to defeat them!

The problem with this particular campaign charge, of course, is that it's just not true. It's a lie. Not only is it a lie, but every single candidate who has made this charge against his opponent *knew*, or should have known, it to be a lie. In our book, that makes these candidates bold, intentional, premeditated liars. Imagine that!

We, your humble authors, have been studying the idea behind the FairTax—funding our federal government with a consumption tax—for twenty years. We are convinced that this plan, to replace virtually all personal and corporate taxes with a consumption tax, would bring a period of transformation and economic growth to America such as has never been seen before. As you have learned, we're far from alone in that belief.

You've already read how the FairTax would work to bring American corporations and businesses back home. Later we'll show you how passing the FairTax Act would bring trillions of expatriated American dollars back home as well. Well, here's another benefit of the FairTax: It would create a financial bonanza for the poor and the middle class. Of course, we don't expect our opponents to be any more honest in this debate than they were in the last election. So we'll have to address the charge ourselves.

Okay . . . let's put on our sensitivity hats for a few minutes here and think of the consequences of the FairTax. The first thing to remember is that, for the most part, Americans living below the poverty line aren't paying income tax anyway. In fact, many of them are getting checks from the government. The absurdly named Earned Income Tax Credit[1] is a prime conduit for income redistribution from high-income earners to the poor and middle class.

We absolutely recognize that the idea of the FairTax would die a quick and grisly death if its only effect were to hit the poor with a 23 percent sales tax on top of today's prices for a gallon of milk or a loaf of bread. This, in fact, is the disingenous charge that has been leveled by those who fear a loss of power if the FairTax were to be enacted. Thankfully, this scenario would be far removed from reality under the FairTax. As you read on you will learn that the 23 percent FairTax is embedded in the price of retail goods and services, not added to it. The truth is, the FairTax could turn out to be the best poverty-fighting tool devised in this country since the concept of hard work.

Let's begin by considering two realities.

First, remember that the poor—along with everybody else—will no longer have Social Security taxes or Medicare taxes withheld from their paychecks. Whatever they earn, they get on payday. If employers leave this money in paychecks instead of taking it out of price, most of those we

---

1. The EITC was passed to relieve lower-income Americans of the tax they pay for Social Security and Medicare. They are already relieved of the responsibility of paying income taxes to pay for our defense, parks, courts, FBI, housing, education—well, everything. So why should they be expected to pay for their retirement programs? This little piece of our budget has grown to $38 billion and it is estimated that over 25 percent of that is fraud.

categorize as poor would see an immediate 25 to 30 percent increase in their take-home pay.

Second, remember that even more taxes are already inflating the retail prices we all pay in the form of embedded taxes buried in the cost of all consumer goods. As soon as the competitive forces of the free market work their magic, as they always do, consumers of all incomes will be paying less for virtually everything they buy, including the basics of food, clothing, shelter, and transportation. Yes, they'll have to pay the new national sales tax—but when you factor in the combined lower prices/higher take-home pay caused by the disappearance of the embedded taxes, you'll see that the total price paid for consumer goods will remain very nearly the same.

So . . . just considering these factors, and these factors alone, the FairTax delivers a winning hand to people living below or near the poverty line. They get every penny they earn on payday—and, when you factor in the FairTax and the lower prices, they'll actually be spending less of their money for a retail purchase than before.

To get a handle on how this would play out, pull out your calculator. Let's say that a single mother with two children spends $45 a week on groceries. The removal of the 22 percent embedded tax would bring the price of those groceries down to $35.10. Add the FairTax, and the groceries would cost $45.58—just a few pennies more. But remember, under the FairTax Plan, this single mother with two children now gets to take home 100 percent of her paycheck. If employers fail to take taxes out of price, the addition of formerly-withheld income taxes and payroll taxes to her paycheck will give her a 25 to 30 percent increase in take-home pay . . . and in exchange she'll pay 23 cents to the tax man in every dollar spent. Does that sound like such a rotten deal to you?

But that's not the half of it.

The folks who wrote the FairTax Plan knew that burdening the poor with a 23 percent retail sales tax would doom the plan from the outset. And since the FairTax was designed from scratch—as opposed to the current hodgepodge of rules and regulations we call "the income tax"—its creators ensured that no one should ever have to pay the sales tax on the basic necessities of life. That's why the prebate—the monthly check covering taxes on all basic household necessities—was invented.

The size of the monthly prebate payment will be based on the government's published poverty levels for various-sized households. The number is updated every year to keep up with inflation, so the work of calculating the size of the prebate is already done. Here's an example of how the prebate payments would work in 2006.

Let's say your household consists of a married couple with two children. The FairTax Act sets forth a formula for computing the poverty level, based on government figures, which negates any marriage penalty. Under the FairTax Act, in 2006 your household would be granted an annual consumption allowance of $26,400. This is the amount the government estimates you would spend during that one year to buy the basic necessities of life for your family. The sales tax on this amount would equal $6,072. The government would rebate this amount to you in twelve equal monthly installments of just under $506.

Now, it's clear that low-income Americans will be better off, *much* better off, under the FairTax Plan. They would have their income and payroll taxes abolished; they would have the 22 percent tax costs that are currently embedded in everything that they buy eliminated; *and* they would receive a payment each month to guarantee that they could spend all of their money up to the poverty level and not lose one penny to taxes. Wow.

To take some other examples: A single woman struggling to raise one child would collect a monthly rebate in 2006 of $253. The lowest rebate payment would go to a single person with no dependents: such a person would receive $188 per month, or $2,254 for the year. Here's a table that spells out the range of prebates available to all Americans:

TABLE 9.1 2006 Spending and Rebates in H.R. 25

| Family | FairTax Poverty Level | | Prebate | |
Size	Annual	Monthly	Monthly	Annual
Single	9,800.00	817.00	188.00	2,254.00
Married	19,600.00	1,633.00	376.00	4,508.00
3	23,000.00	1,917.00	441.00	5,290.00
4	26,400.00	2,200.00	506.00	6,072.00
5	29,800.00	2,483.00	571.00	6,854.00
6	33,200.00	2,767.00	636.00	7,636.00
7	36,600.00	3,050.00	702.00	8,418.00
8	40,000.00	3,333.00	767.00	9,200.00
Each additional family member	3,400.00	283.00	65.00	782.00

Now . . . bear in mind, the prebate isn't just for the poor. It's paid to everyone, rich and poor alike. The purpose here is to make sure that no American has to pay the FairTax on the basic necessities of life. Unlike the present income tax system, the FairTax treats each and every person in this country exactly the same. This, of course, presents something of a problem to politicians who like to use the tax code to foment class distrust or outright warfare.

Sorry, but if you're looking for some reason to oppose the FairTax Plan, you're going to have to find a better excuse than its effect on the poor.

The politicians who are using sponsorship of the FairTax proposal against their opponents know the real story. They also know that for the most part the media doesn't understand the plan—and in most cases hasn't yet made any effort to learn the truth. That's why we're doing this book—and that's why we want you to tell your friends about it. (Besides all those extra sales for us!) It's important to expose the lies of those who are trying to paint the FairTax as an attack on the poor. This tax reform idea is simply too good to allow it to be destroyed by the lies of those who gain from the complexity of the current tax system.

An aside: We don't want to get into the Democrat vs. Republican thing in this book, so we'll just tell you of what happened in one particular race for the U.S. Senate in 2004. No names, no party affiliations . . . just the facts. In this particular state, there was one national party (go ahead, guess if you like, you'll probably be right) that spent more than $4 million on TV ads condemning the other party's candidate for supporting the FairTax. The ad said that the evil So-and-So wanted to add a new 23 percent sales tax to the price of everything you buy. No details other than that. The ad was, simply put, dishonest. The FairTax supporter won that election, and exit polls showed that 25 percent of the voters cast their votes that day believing that "taxes" was the most important issue in the election. Guess what? Among that 25 percent, two out of every three votes was for the FairTax supporter. It's comforting to know that so many of the voters in this particular state saw right through the $4 million in campaign lies and rhetoric . . . and showed their support for the FairTax at the polls.

The truth is that those in the lowest income levels in our society should be the ones out there campaigning the hardest for the FairTax. For them it's all benefit and no burden. After paying for their basic necessities without any taxation at all, they'll have money left over to invest in their future, through savings accounts, courses at the local community college, or other means. Perhaps this is what frightens some politicians. When the poor start to invest in their own futures, when they start to save for their own retirements, they slowly but surely become financially independent. As hard as you may find this to believe, there are some politicians out there who thrive on dependency. You'll be able to recognize them by their opposition to the FairTax.

Now, hold on, you may be thinking. *Is government really up to the challenge of making the FairTax prebate payments?* Well, consider this: Our federal government already sends out nearly 48 million checks a month to Social Security recipients alone. Add to that the checks that go to federal employees, federal retirees, federal contractors, and so on, and you can see that the government is a check-writing machine. (No surprise, is it?) You don't want to know how much that used to cost in postage! Thankfully (after all, this book is supposed to be uplifting, not depressing), most of these payments are delivered electronically today. But the government does issue these payments, and by all accounts it does so rather effectively. We submit to you that any government that is already issuing 48 million checks covering Social Security recipients alone won't have that big a problem issuing FairTax rebates to every head of household in this country.

Here's how it might roll out: Let's say the FairTax Act has become law, and the implementation date is around the corner. Every head of household would be asked to file one simple report with the government. It could be a household of one—you. Or maybe you're a household of eight: you, your wife, and your six wonderful, well-behaved children. All you need to do is list the name and Social Security number of everyone living under your roof. (Why provide your Social Security number? Sadly, there are some people in this country who might try to scam the system and receive more than one rebate check. To prevent this, the government would use computers to match and compare Social Security numbers to catch those with plunder in their hearts.)

Once the names of heads of household are assembled, it would be a simple matter for the government to create the database of those who will receive the monthly rebates.

And it might be even easier than sending out physical checks. Consider this possibility: a FairTax Card! The government could issue such a card to every head of household who has registered with the federal government. This FairTax Card would be much like your bank debit card, with a magnetic stripe identifying you and coded with your PIN.

Once the cards are issued, it would take a simple mouse click in Washington for your FairTax Card to be credited with your monthly rebate payment. You then go forth into the retail marketplace using your FairTax Card as cash until it's depleted for that month—all the while leaving the money you've actually earned resting comfortably in your interest-bearing and tax-free checking or savings account. ("Interest-bearing and tax-free"—don't you love the way that sounds?)

All your monthly bills, paid with one click of the mouse. What could be better?

10

UNDERGROUND AND OFFSHORE ECONOMY . . . TAXED AT LAST!

Income tax returns are the most imaginative fiction being written today.

—Herman Wouk

The income tax has made more liars out of the American people than golf has.

—Will Rogers

Now that you have a basic understanding of the workings of the FairTax, let's cover some of the problems that will be solved when we finally move our country away from a tax system that punishes achievement. We're going to talk about tax evasion, the underground economy, the shadow economy, and offshore financial centers (OFCs). Add up the effects of these economic realities, and the cost in tax revenues runs into hundreds of billions of dollars.

The Greeks knew the truth two thousand years before the American Revolution. As the great philosopher Plato wrote in *The Republic* during the fourth century BC, "Where there is an income tax, the just man will pay more and the unjust less on the same amount of income." True to Plato's wisdom, Americans have lived "off the books" since we have imposed the income tax. In the beginning, the tax code skimmed only a small percentage off the incomes of the very top earners—taxpayers rich enough that they had little incentive to avoid taxes. It was only when the income tax started to affect nearly every American—and the burden on high achievers became particularly onerous—that schemes for tax evasion proliferated.

Most Americans probably think that tax evaders are generally people who make their livings outside of the law—criminals, drug dealers, money launderers, prostitutes, and the like. The reality? You—yeah, you—are probably playing the same game they are. Here's how.

If your maid, gardener, home repairman, or house painter asks to be paid in cash—or is, perhaps, in our country illegally—and you cooperate, you're aiding in tax evasion. If you buy a hot dog from a vendor on our city streets, it's a pretty good bet you're doing cash business with someone who's not reporting all of his income. For that matter, the same could be said of many of the servers in our restaurants—in spite of the withholding laws, which force some of the responsibility for reporting their cash income on their employer.

Let's face it: We Americans cheat on our taxes! And when we do, we become part of the "shadow economy"—that is, the world of legal activities that are not reported for tax purposes. Add to this figure the "underground economy," the world of illegal activities—drug dealers, hookers, and the like—and the magnitude of the problem becomes clear.

A 2000 survey concluded that our shadow economy accounts for more than 10 percent of America's GDP—that's a huge hunk. And the major force behind this shadow economy? Taxes. More specifically, according to the study, the "increasing burden of taxation and Social Security payments, combined with rising state regulatory activities and labor market restrictions (e.g., forced reduction in working hours)."[1] The IRS calls this figure the "tax gap," and concludes that it grows every year. Most recently, the IRS reported this figure at $345 billion in lost tax revenues.

There may be a part of you that says, "Well, good for them! They've managed to find a way to avoid getting shafted by the government. I only wish I could figure out how to do it myself." Well, you may not realize it, but these tax avoiders are taking money right out of your pocket. Think about it. It's not like the government just allows that $345 billion to slip away unnoticed. Lose a little money here,

---

1. Friedrich Schneider and Dominik H. Enste, "Shadow Economies: Size, Causes, and Consequences," *Journal of Economic Literature,* 38 (March 2000), pp. 77–114. Schneider and Enste define the shadow economy as legal income-producing activities that are not reported to tax authorities and do not include illegal activities.

and the logical thing is to recover it there—and *there,* for the government, means *your wallet.* Each of the 150 million American taxpayers pays an average of $2,000 extra every year to the IRS to cover the missing revenue. Still think it's "good for them"? Even when it's so bad for you?

The government has a variety of means it can use to estimate the amount of taxes it loses to unreported income. One simple way is by comparing the amount of income declared on personal tax returns to the amount of personal consumption during any given year. Another way is to measure the demand for currency in our economy.

If you happen to have a U.S. $100 bill in your wallet right now, take it out and look at it. You are holding what has become the international currency for illegal behavior. Today, nearly three-quarters of all $100 bills circulate outside of the United States. Criminals like to hold their wealth in hundreds. Actually, this works to the benefit of the United States in a rather odd way. When the U.S. Treasury issues new banknotes, including $100 bills, it purchases an equal value of interest-bearing securities to cover the notes. When those banknotes are taken out of circulation, the government must pay off those securities, together with earned interest. So when three-quarters of all $100 bills are being secreted outside the United States, the Treasury Department saves money. How? As long as those bills remain in circulation, the government doesn't have to pay off the securities issued to cover them. How much does that save us? Try about $32.7 billion in interest in the year 2000 alone.[2]

---

2. Eric Schlosser, *Reefer Madness,* Mariner Books, 2004.

(And get this: When the European Union wanted some of this action, it introduced the 500 euro note—an attempt to grab some of the $100 bill business away from America.)

By tracing changes in the demand for currency, Austrian economist Friedrich Schneider estimated that the size of the underground economy in 1970 was approximately 2.6 to 4.6 percent of the American GDP. By 1994, it had reached 9.4 percent—approximately $650 billion. These are earnings that aren't getting taxed—and you're making up the difference.

Charles Rossotti, the former commissioner of the IRS, estimated that Americans avoided reporting almost $1.5 trillion in personal income in 1998. This did not include undeclared earnings from criminal activity, because the IRS has no reliable data to use in estimating that. We know the criminal figures are astronomical, however. Eric Schlosser, a correspondent for the *Atlantic Monthly,* estimates in his wonderfully thorough book *Reefer Madness* that just three components of the underground economy—illicit drugs, illegal labor, and pornography—constitute an economy that exceeds $1 trillion.

It is widely agreed that the underground economy is huge, and that most of the growth has occurred in the past thirty years. This growth stems largely from a growing sense of anger and alienation over a government that seems to insist that what we produce is theirs, and that we should be allowed to keep no more than our politicians decide we deserve. Perhaps you remember some elected officials who were opposed to President Bush's tax cuts—politicians who were upset because, they claimed, the people who were going to benefit the most from the cuts didn't actually "need" the money. We don't know about you, but many Americans are a bit troubled by the prospect of politicians determining just how much of our hard-earned money we actually "need." Isn't that for us to decide?

Here's a sobering fact: The government has a name—a label, if you will—for that portion of your earnings that you manage, by using standard tax deductions, to keep for your own uses instead of handing it over to the IRS. What name is that? Get this: They call it "tax expenditures." How do you like that—the government considers the portion of your earnings that you are allowed to keep to be an "expenditure" that actually belonged to the government in the first place. Sorry, but isn't that a little difficult to swallow?

Of course, none of this is meant to suggest that any underground-economy activities would be legalized by passage of the FairTax. Nor would it become more visible or reported. But this much is true: Under the FairTax Plan, criminals will pay their taxes every time they spend their money on personal consumption—after all, even criminals and other tax evaders like to eat, buy homes, and drive nice cars.

The key point here is that the increasing complexity of the tax code increases the size of the underground economy. Increasing complexity makes taxes easier to avoid, and the increasing burden on the IRS makes it less likely that the avoidance will be discovered.

So far, we have been discussing only those who avoid taxes by nefarious means. But there's an even larger tax-avoidance drag on our economy: those who avoid taxes absolutely legally. That's right, the abomination that is our confiscatory tax code is also largely responsible for driving trillions (with a capital "T") of dollars into offshore financial centers. These dollars are then effectively sheltered from any participation in the American economy. There are several reasons for this, and we'll examine them, but here is the important number: the 2000 Merrill Lynch & Gemini Consulting study *World Wealth Report* estimates that one-third of the wealth of the world's high-net-worth individuals is held offshore. How much would that be? Try $11 trillion—$11 trillion sucked out of the American economy, all of it immune to the tax obligations you suffer every April 15.[3]

This began for the simplest of reasons. In the 1950s, the former Soviet Union was doing a great deal of business in the West. They were eager to hold U.S. dollars, because our economy was more stable and our markets more liquid. They also wanted to use dollars to pay for the routine bills they had incurred in the United States. Some of the obligations were simply bills for purchases from American suppliers. Others were for paying spies and arms merchants. In the underworld of the Cold War—just as in today's underworld—the currency of choice is the American dollar.

But the Soviets didn't want to hold those dollars in America for fear that they would be confiscated by the American government in a "showdown." The communist leaders knew

---

3. Cut this amount in half, and it still exceeds the GDP of every nation on the planet except the United States.

that the United States had foreclosed on bank accounts of tyrants in the past, and they didn't want to risk that happening to them.

The Soviets approached British banks with their dilemma, and the British began allowing depositors in their banks to hold their money in U.S. dollars. Thus was born the Eurodollar market. "Eurodollars"[4] are American dollars held by foreign banks or by foreign branches of American banks. Depositing their dollars outside of the United States allows the holders of Eurodollars to escape regulation by the Federal Reserve Board. Originally, such dollar-denominated foreign deposits were held almost exclusively in Europe. These deposits are now held in such countries as the Bahamas, Canada, the Cayman Islands, Hong Kong, Japan, the Netherlands Antilles, Panama, and Singapore—but they're still universally referred to as Eurodollars.

Since the Eurodollar market is relatively free of regulation, banks in the market can operate on narrower margins than banks in the United States. Thus, the Eurodollar market has expanded largely as a means of avoiding the regulatory costs involved in dollar-denominated financial intermediation.

The next expansion of offshore banking came at the behest of the American government. We were fighting a war in Vietnam, but our government didn't want to raise taxes to pay for it, so it was decided that we should encourage our

---

4. Not to be confused with euros, the currency of the European Union.

banks to expand into offshore banking to attract foreign capital into dollars. It worked. The policy was successful in turning U.S. banks into a flight-capital center for third-world dictators, Russian oligarchs, Mexican presidents, and illegal "hot money" from around the globe. Well, it didn't take too many years before international corporations recognized the benefits of keeping deposits in Eurodollars for other reasons.

Many government decisions fall victim to the laws of unintended consequences. The British and American decisions that created the Eurodollar market have left us, fifty years later, with a totally private banking system for international corporations, high-net-worth individuals, and illegal operators. This system of offshore financial centers is safe, secure, and secret, and it operates outside of the political borders and regulatory authority of the United States. It has become a magnet for illegal money, and a "safe harbor" for those who wish to avoid paying taxes on money lawfully earned.

Our government estimates that it loses at least $100 billion each year in unpaid tax collections due to Eurodollar transactions. Between 1989 and 1995, more than half of all corporations doing business in the United States, both foreign and domestic controlled, paid no U.S. income tax.

Offshore financial centers have grown into a sophisticated draw on American capital, with many uses:

1. A multinational corporation may set up its own OFC bank to deal with many administrative aspects of its business. Such a bank can be used to pay for account-

ing, administration, investments, currency trades, and other functions, with little or no tax consequences and less stringent reporting and trading restrictions.

2. OFCs are used to set up international business corporations (IBCs), which are popular (because generally tax- and regulation-free) vehicles for managing investment funds.

3. Insurance companies use OFCs for reinsuring catastrophic risks, which often have lower actuarial requirements and capital standards. They also make great places to recognize profits.

4. Wealthy individuals use OFCs to protect assets and for tax planning. (And no, they don't pay the death tax.)

5. Foreign wealth is often kept in OFCs, to be protected from weak banking systems.

6. Tax evasion and money laundering schemes are difficult to track down in OFCs.

Using OFCs is also a convenient way to keep questionable funds—funds from the underground or shadow economy—accessible. The International Monetary Fund estimates that between $600 billion and $1.5 trillion in illicit profit is laundered annually. The vast majority of that is laundered offshore. If a criminal stashes his ill-gotten gains in one of these OFCs, all he needs is a simple debit card issued by that offshore bank to access his funds. Based on MasterCard records obtained by an IRS summons, it's estimated that one to two million Americans are using such accounts.

There are some fifty-five offshore banking locales.[5] Switzerland and the Cayman Islands[6] are legendary among them, of course. Behind the Cayman Islands comes Nauru in the South Pacific. Nauru has only ten thousand residents, but it has four hundred offshore banks.

Any nation that hosts these OFCs has the legal right to levy—or not levy—a tax at any stage in the recognition of wealth, capital gains, or income. That fact gives corporations and individuals who are banking in OFCs the choice of recognizing their profit in the lowest-taxed jurisdiction available.

The oil industry learned this long ago. For nearly one hundred years, the oil industry has been carrying its oil to the United States—and other nations—on ships that fly the flag of low-tax nations. Liberia and Panama, which levy *no* taxes, have most often been cited as "homes" to these ships. The oil companies have the option of recognizing the vast majority of their gains in one of those nations with little or no tax on income or capital gains. They then send the product to its final consumer in America—where the profit on the final transaction, and the attendant taxes, are negligible.

Enron, the notorious energy giant, received a significant amount of bad publicity for the "offshore partnerships" it created for the purpose of recognizing profits in jurisdictions with lower taxes and less regulation. Enron was not alone.

---

5. To facilitate offshore banking, forty-seven of these countries and jurisdictions have "dollarized" or "euroized" their currency—meaning that the dollar or the euro is an official currency of the land.
6. Cayman is the fifth largest financial center in the world.

Virtually every major corporation also participates offshore. Small companies are now moving into the game for the same reason. By merely having a lawyer on the selected island fill out the necessary paperwork, you are a company with a foreign presence.

Fifty years ago, corporate America contributed approximately one-third of all the income taxes collected by the federal government. Today, that number is about 10 percent. That plunge is a major factor in our recent soaring deficits. Indeed, international corporations are essentially "voluntary" taxpayers today, paying only that amount in taxes that they believe will avoid attracting embarrassing news coverage. These corporations believe that our draconian tax structures make their actions necessary. The OFCs make their plans feasible.

Okay, we've spent several pages burying you with the scoop on OFCs—information you might think has nothing to do with the subject at hand: the FairTax. Well, if that's what you think, you're missing the point.

There have been many proposals designed to find a way to tax these Eurodollars and offshore accounts, and allow the government to start collecting money more efficiently from these corporations. A decade ago, a growing number of Americans were giving up their U.S. citizenship and becoming citizens of Ireland or the Bahamas because of America's punishing inheritance tax. The response was to try to grab their bank accounts before they got out of town. Opponents of the grab-the-cash-before-they-leave plan responded by saying, "They are not leaving because they hate us. They are leaving because our tax code is chasing them away."

Today, we see regular debates in Congress about those people who are relocating their business headquarters outside of our country. Some have proposed prohibiting these corporations from participation in any federal contracts. Others have proposed granting some measure of trade favoritism to nations that would make the transactions less secret.

Why punish American corporations, and thus their customers and employees, for using perfectly legal means to avoid paying America's burdensome taxes? There is a better idea, you know. It's called the FairTax.

If we eliminated all taxes on capital and labor, as the FairTax does, the United States would become the world's tax haven. We have the most stable economy, the most liquid and trusted markets, and the highest rates of labor productivity in the world—and the trillions of dollars in those OFCs would flow back home to the United States for the very reason they found themselves offshore to start with.

Not only would the estranged American dollars come back home, but many trillions more from foreign nations would flow into the United States for the very same reasons. Having no IRS or reporting requirements would give those with wealth—no matter where they're from—the security, safety, and secrecy they seek. That money would go into our financial centers to be available to loan for lower interest rates. These loans would create new businesses and expand old ones—and, in so doing, would create jobs. As the money from the underground and shadow economies came home to America, our own economy would be the beneficiary.

Remember, right now about $11 trillion in American wealth is sitting in banks and accounts in Europe, Asia, South America, the Caribbean, and elsewhere. This is money that is not working in the American economy. This is money that is not creating jobs and driving economic growth in our country. This is money that has fled our punishing tax structure, and that would come flowing back home if the income tax, both personal and corporate, were to be eliminated and replaced with a simple and fair consumption tax: the FairTax.

11

SO WE'VE DONE IT. WHAT HAPPENS TO OUR ECONOMY?

> Our present tax system...exerts too heavy a drag on growth...It reduces the financial incentives for personal effort, investment, and risk-taking...the present tax load...distorts economic judgments and channels an undue amount of energy into efforts to avoid tax liabilities.
>
> —John F. Kennedy, November 20, 1962

So let's say the FairTax is adopted tomorrow. What happens to the American economy? Before asking that question, it might be better to start by remembering what the current system does *to* the economy. We have some huge economic forces coming into play that will shape our children's world. We spent $265 billion in 2005 filling out IRS paperwork.

Businessmen and -women will tell you that we spend that much time and money calculating the tax implications of a business decision. Wasted money. Wasted time. To spend more than $400 billion to collect just three times that much in tax revenues is not only inefficient, it's completely dumb.

So back to the question: What happens after the income tax is gone and the FairTax becomes our reality? There are a hundred little answers, but the one big answer is the most important: *growth*.

Economists estimate that in the first year after the FairTax Act becomes law, the economy will grow by 10.5 percent. Exports will grow by 26 percent. And capital spending will increase by more than 70 percent. Increases in capital spending make the American worker more productive, and their paychecks increase in exact correspondence with that spending.

Want more? Fine. How about declining interest rates? Some models suggest a decline of as much as 30 percent! Think of how much easier it will be for average Americans to afford a new home or automobile once they're collecting 100 percent of their earnings and interest rates are declining. As the economy increases in size, so will federal revenues from the consumption tax. Crunching the numbers, we find that if the United States had been operating under the FairTax, government revenues would have increased in fifteen of the past sixteen quarters. That translates into lower federal deficits and a reduced national debt.

The $400 to $500 billion we spend today just complying with the IRS would be additional dollars in our pockets— available to spend, to invest, or to use in creating jobs. This would be the equivalent of a $4 trillion tax cut over ten years, without cutting government revenues one penny—now, that's not a bad deal! In 2003, Congress spent an entire summer haggling over a ten-year tax cut worth $330 billion. Opponents whined that the proposal "gave" too much to the "rich."[1] Our $4 trillion will go straight into the pockets of American consumers, to spend or save as they see fit. This will provide a tremendous economic boost to the American people and to our country.

Let's revisit that $11 trillion in offshore accounts. When the income tax is repealed, and all that wealth comes back to our own financial institutions, much of that $11 trillion will end up in our markets, increasing the value of stocks and bonds. Other repatriated dollars will find their way into our banks and credit unions, leading to that fall in interest rates. Still other returning dollars will be used to build new businesses and create new jobs.

The underground economy, which currently escapes taxes on about $1.5 trillion, would no longer enjoy its tax-free status. The illegal activities in which they engage would not be legalized, but every retail purchase the criminals made—whether a mochachino or a Mercedes—would be taxed the same as yours and mine.

The single largest category of "escapees" from taxes, of course, is bankruptcy. Yes, Americans would still be able to

---

1. The talk show host can't help interjecting here: How absurd is it when you hear the tax-and-spend crowd whine about how tax cuts "give" money to the wealthy? *Give?* Since when does allowing a person to keep more of his or her hard-earned money constitute "giving" that person anything? Giving them a break . . . maybe.

avoid their financial obligations through bankruptcy—but when they walked out of the federal courthouse after that bankruptcy hearing and headed for the nearest restaurant, they would be right back to paying taxes the moment the check came.

Consider this: The single largest category of IRS legal actions are brought against businesses, most of them small businesses, that collect the FICA tax from their employees but fail to remit those dollars to the Treasury. With the Fair-Tax Plan, this is no longer a problem because there's no more withholding scheme to exploit. Now these businesses can concentrate on the job at hand, growing their business, instead of keeping payroll records for Uncle Sam.

Then there's the matter of personal savings and investments. According to recent news reports, the personal savings rate in the United States is at an all-time low. People are spending their money, not saving it. Economists are unanimous in their belief that an increase in the personal savings rate is key to a growing and robust economy. Virtually every economic study on the FairTax proposal concludes that people from one end of the economic spectrum to the other—from the poor to the very rich—will either start a savings and investment plan or increase the one they already have.

Finally, let's consider the global implications of the Fair-Tax. We've already described the 22 percent worth of tax and compliance costs embedded in our price system thanks to the current IRS system. Under the FairTax Plan, those costs disappear, making your purchases cost about the same even with the FairTax added back in. But equally important is the drop in the cost of American goods in a global economy. If our corporations were the only companies that could sell into a global economy with *no* embedded tax component in our pricing system, no one could compete with us.

To remain competitive, foreign corporations will be compelled to build new plants in America so that they too can go about their businesses without suffering taxes on capital and labor. As with American companies, this will make their businesses more competitive in the global economy. As foreign business operations move facilities to America, foreign leaders will take notice. These leaders will be forced to choose between competing head to head against America and its FairTax economy, or suffer the negative consequences of a failure to compete. And just how would you compete with our FairTax economy? Easy! Just get the full tax component out of the prices for your manufactured goods, by doing what they did in America: enacting their own version of the FairTax. Soon the forward-thinking nations of the world will be getting rid of all business taxes, compliance costs, payroll and income taxes—and then stand back!

Let's put it another way. To compete with America in the global market, other countries will have to recognize that the best way to economic prosperity is to allow people to be free in their economic endeavors—to make whatever voluntary arrangements they choose, with *whomever* they choose, *whenever* they choose, without constraint from unfair tax consequences. That has huge implications for the world economy, and for the cause of freedom.

As Nobel laureate Milton Friedman wrote in 1962, "Freedom in economic arrangements is itself a component of freedom broadly understood, so economic freedom is an end in itself. . . . Economic freedom is also an indispensable means toward the achievement of political freedom."[2]

As other nations turn their constituents into "voluntary" taxpayers by copying us, they will also eliminate the coercive nature of their tax collection system and allow economic freedom to expand throughout the world. More than anything we can think of, that would spread freedom across the globe!

Now, don't just take our word for this. Let's turn to the experts. In 1997, Congress's Joint Tax Committee began to explore what a fundamental reform of the tax code would look like and what effect it would have on our economy. The Committee discovered it didn't even have a valid model to predict the outcome, because the Committee's models were all designed to nibble around the edges of the tax code. So the Committee called in teams of economic experts to model the impact on our economy of replacing the income tax with a consumption tax. What did these teams of economic experts discover? Every one of those nine teams found that a consumption tax would grow the economy faster than the current system. From liberals to conservatives, every economic team recognized the drag the current system places on our economy. While some of these experts felt that the growth would be rapid and others believed growth would only occur more slowly over time, everyone believed a consumption tax would grow the economy faster than any growth we would experience under the present system.

And remember: Economic growth is economist-speak for *jobs, jobs, jobs.*

---

2. Milton Friedman, *Capitalism and Freedom* (Chicago: University of Chicago Press, 1962).

Time for a Quick Review!

Here's what happens when we pass and implement the FairTax Plan:

- We start controlling our earnings in every paycheck.
- We all start receiving monthly prebates equal to the amount of consumption tax we would be expected to pay on life's basic necessities.
- We all start saving and investing without any tax consequences.
- Our purchasing power for buying consumer goods and services remains essentially the same, with the removal of the embedded taxes compensating for the added consumption tax.
- American businesses return operations to their home turf.
- The richest Americans bring their money back home where it helps fuel our economy.
- Those operating in the underground and shadow economies finally start paying taxes.
- You hear the unmistakable voice of that IRS agent who audited you three years ago asking if you'd like fries with that.

The FairTax: What's not to love?

12

THE OPPOSITION. WHERE WILL IT COME FROM?

Even though the idea of replacing our current income tax structure with a consumption tax has been around for generations, and the FairTax has been around for quite a few years, until recently there's really been no organized opposition to the idea. Why now? The reason is clear. The FairTax is finally receiving serious consideration in Washington, and those who think they might be hurt by the proposal are beginning to take notice.

It would be easy in this chapter to name names, to call those opposed to the FairTax out of their foxholes to fight with us out in the open where everyone can watch. The talk-show guy likes this approach—after all, that's basically how he makes his living. Between these covers, however, cooler heads have prevailed. The supporters of the FairTax are engaged in active talks with the few opposing groups there are, so we'll try not to "out" them in this book . . . though the talk-show half of this writing team has already done so on his program. He promises to cool the rhetoric . . . at least for a while.

Is the FairTax really taking hold? Let's just say one highly placed lobbyist was recently quoted as saying that a few years ago this whole FairTax idea was just a proposal from an "obscure" Georgia congressman.[1] Now, sayeth the lobbyist, the majority leader of the House and the president of the United States are talking about the FairTax. So, presumably, it's time to take up arms and ride to the battle.

There will be fierce opposition to the FairTax, and the worst of it will likely come from Washington, D.C. Thousands of people who used to work on Capitol Hill now find themselves working on K Street (the lobbyists' habitat), making unimaginable sums of money gaming the current tax system. Their intellectual capital is their knowledge of the tax code. But their value will be substantially depreciated with the passage of the FairTax. They aren't exactly thrilled with the prospect.

---

1. The Georgia congressman wishes, for the record, to show that he is hurt by this representation, and further states for the record that he has never considered himself to be obscure. Obtuse, maybe . . . but never obscure.

Remember what we said earlier—that the percentage of federal tax revenue paid by corporate America has fallen from 30 percent to about 10 percent? This apparent magic is the work of the folks from K Street, who have been paid huge sums to gain advantages for their corporate clients—advantages that come at your expense.

Let's create a hypothetical organization to illustrate our point. (Starting all these businesses is fun, isn't it?) We'll call this one the American Association of Electronics Manufacturers (AAEM). This association has twelve thousand members and an operating budget of $62 million a year, which is covered entirely by its member companies. The president of the AAEM is a former congressman, now pulling in a million-dollar salary to work for the electronics manufacturers. (This is no exaggeration, by the way—such salaries are common on K Street.) The AAEM has a staff of more than two hundred in Washington. The AAEM's member companies would be among the biggest beneficiaries of the FairTax, because the plan would enable them to sell into a global economy with no embedded taxes hiking up their prices.

Yet the AAEM staff actively opposes the FairTax!

Here's why.

Virtually every year, Congress deals with tax code changes. Think back to 1986, the year when our tax code was "simplified" by getting rid of tax deductions and then lowering taxes with just a few flat tax brackets. Good try. Since 1986, that simplification of our tax code has been amended *more than ten thousand times*. Every one of those amendments was the work of some proponent, somewhere, pushing some senator or congressman to do his interest group's tax amendment.

And you can bet this much: Somewhere along the way, someone made money.

After any major tax overhaul (like the 1986 Tax Reform Act), the president of the AAEM and his top economic advisers and lobbyists meet with the membership at their annual meeting. (Look for them in Maui, let's say; the whole trip would be written off as a tax-deductible business expense.) The board of AAEM would be told by the Washington office that they might be able to influence some tax code changes that would save AAEM members about $12 billion in taxes over the next five years. *"Aren't we special?"* the lobbyists would say. *"Now do you see why you pay us those big salaries?"* Think about this, though. If the FairTax passes, eliminating taxes on businesses—along with the burden of considering tax implications before making business decisions—who's going to need tax lobbyists? The Washington office would have to keep some people on just to watch over the regulatory burden of government, but no more worries about the tax code!

The folks who sell houses—and we mean both realtors in your neighborhood and the people down the street putting their place on the market—know that they'll do better under the FairTax Plan. *(Shall we go through that exercise again? Houses will cost slightly less because the embedded tax cost of 23 percent is slightly less than the current embedded cost of the IRS on new construction. If you're making $60,000 per year, you're currently taking home $3,800 per month to pay your mortgage and other bills. Under the FairTax, you'll take home $5,000—*

and you'll pay less in interest because rates will decline by about 30 percent.)

With lower interest rates, higher savings rates, and more disposable income, it's clear that both home sellers and home builders will benefit from the implementation of the FairTax. But what will the national lobbying arms of these groups do when faced with passage of the FairTax? They'll fight to the last person. And why? Because these trade associations have spent decades working toward essentially one goal: to protect the deductibility of mortgage interest payments. If there's no income tax, and thus nothing to deduct from, how will they continue to justify their expensive existence?[2]

As you read this, you can bet that the lobbyists and advisers are already joining forces on K Street. They're our opposition: the people who make the big bucks off the hideous complexity of our present tax system and, in the process, inhibit economic growth while keeping their boots on the necks of individual American taxpayers. Every lobbyist in Washington who needs to protect his big salary will be taking his or her shot at the FairTax.

These opposing organizations will stoke the fires and raise a smokescreen on three issues. Here are a few of their favorite arguments:

- First, they'll claim that a tax on consumption would create a new wave of sales tax evasion, thus giving rise to large black markets.

---

2. The question of the deductibility of home mortgage interest will be addressed more thoroughly in chapter 15 on frequently asked questions.

- Second, they'll claim that the transition costs would be unbearable.
- And third, they'll claim that the FairTax is "regressive"—the Washington buzzword for "hurts the poor."

Let's look at these arguments one by one.

For years, we've heard FairTax opponents contend that they have studies purportedly proving that any sales tax above 10 percent would lead to widespread avoidance. A huge underground economy would develop, they argue, as countless Americans try to avoid paying sales tax. After repeated requests, however, no one has ever presented a study that proves this point.

Now, there's no reason not to be realistic here. Plenty of people will try to avoid paying this tax. As we said before. . . . We Americans cheat on taxes! It's almost a part of our culture. But how easy will it be to cheat?

Most analysts agree that under the current system the IRS collects roughly 75 percent of the taxes owed. The director of the IRS recently said that in 2001 Americans avoided paying $290 billion in taxes they owed—even after the IRS made huge increases in staff and policing. Not surprisingly, most of this avoidance comes from small businesses and personal taxable transactions. There is some agreement that between $1 trillion and $1.5 trillion in the underground economy goes untaxed. It is clear that a taxpayer can lie on his or her tax return and never tell the spouse—and in doing so will run less than a 1 percent chance of being caught.

Under the FairTax, on the other hand, two people must conspire to cheat: The provider or seller, and the consumer or buyer. Now, we don't know how many friends you have who are willing to go to jail to save you 23 cents out of a dollar spent. We certainly don't hang around with people like that!

Will there be avoidance? You bet. But we believe it'll be more difficult under the FairTax. Of course, the K Street crowd will make all the hay they can out of this tax avoidance prospect. Yet it remains the case that 80 percent of the sales tax collections will come from about 20 percent of the businesses—including the national and regional retailers—and I doubt that Wal-Mart or Home Depot or your local hospital is going to risk jail time to help you.

The second argument is the idea that "transition costs" will be unbearable. What might they be? In a meeting some time ago with six of the nation's largest retailers, their representatives claimed that they couldn't sustain the huge costs involved in a transition to the FairTax Plan. When asked exactly what those costs might be, however, all they could come up with was the idea that they would have to replace their point-of-sale cash registers with models set to handle the new tax rate. Were they kidding? "Call me stupid," we said, "but I just assumed your cash registers were electronic." There are 7,500 tax jurisdictions in this country. One or more of them alters its tax rates every week. Do retailers buy new cash registers every week? We don't think so.

The fact is, the FairTax would cause no serious burden on retailers. The real opposition comes from their Washington lobbyists, who are telling their clients they shouldn't have to serve as tax collectors. Of course, they're tax collectors already (remember that embedded 22 percent)? At a corporate level, another thing that apparently scares these retailers is the notion that once that 22 percent automatic price hike disappears, investors looking at yearly sales per store would be confused—leading to a dip in stock prices. Yet surely such investors would know intuitively that the elimination of income taxes, payroll taxes, and compliance costs would have an immensely positive effect on profits. Only their Washington lobbyists would deny that!

Okay, now, let's take a separate paragraph to make this next point—for that matter, why not throw in some bold type and italics? Some retailers and their lobbying organizations are expressing a fear that ***when we all start controlling 100 percent of our earned income in our paychecks—and figure out that we're not being taxed on the money we invest or put into savings accounts—we'll start saving more and not spending every dollar we earn!***

But that, dear friends, is exactly what our economy needs—more personal savings! Do the nation's retailers really want us, especially the poorer among us, to get out there and spend every penny we earn? Are they really so shortsighted that they don't recognize how valuable increased personal savings would be to our economy?

The fact is, the transition cost for retailers will be negligible; the FairTax even provides a payment to the retailers to compensate for this cost. The one transition rule in the bill allows for businesses to use the value of inventory on hand when the bill goes into effect as a credit against collecting the tax in the next year. For example, if you have a million dollars in inventory on December 31, the first million dollars in sales in the next year will not be taxed. (Remember, the principle of the FairTax is that everything should be taxed only once—and that inventory already had the previous year's embedded tax in it.)

Some have suggested that the FairTax Plan will be met with steadfast opposition from accountants and IRS employees. If that's the case, we haven't seen it yet. Many accountants will tell you that they could spend their time performing much more important functions for their clients than watching changes in the tax code and filling out tax returns.

And what about all those IRS employees? We're constantly being asked if the IRS has audited either of us because of our outspoken desire to eliminate their jobs. Actually, the IRS has been almost completely silent on the subject. The political partner in this endeavor reports that he has had one visit from the IRS over this issue. The meeting came about well before the introduction of the actual FairTax legislation, after an IRS official attended a town hall meeting and saw the congressman receive a standing ovation for saying that we should repeal all taxes on income, abolish the IRS, and move to a national sales tax. A donnybrook of discussion followed, with many attendees standing up and sharing their own IRS horror stories.

When the official from the IRS appeared without an appointment in the congressman's district office, he said, "I just showed up hoping you could see me. I didn't give your staff my name. I said I was with the IRS. All of this will make sense when you hear what I want to say." He told the congressman that he was a senior manager in the IRS's nearby regional office. But then he landed his stunner: "I sincerely hope you succeed in your effort to repeal the tax on income and move to a sales tax," he said. "The situation is much worse than you can imagine. The IRS is out of control and needs to be abolished."

Wow! They talked for a while about his experiences, and then he departed. We still don't know his name.

Will there be opposition? Yes, of course there will. It will be vicious, relentless, and disingenuous. Down and dirty. Though it's apparent that the FairTax would clearly benefit the nation as a whole, there will always be narrow special interests eager to destroy such an idea if they feel their own financial situation might be affected. They say that no good deed goes unpunished. Similarly, no good idea goes unopposed.

13

SOCIAL SECURITY
AND MEDICARE
UNDER THE FAIRTAX

This book is about tax reform. We know, though, that the tax reform movement isn't the only such groundswell on the minds of Americans and Beltway politicians. President Bush put a great deal of his political capital behind a push to reform Social Security in 2005. As of this writing, the politicians are still arguing. There's no shortage of evidence that Social Security is on the verge of financial collapse, and Medicare is pretty close to being on life support itself.

If this is a book about reforming our tax system, then why even bring up Social Security and Medicare? First, because the topics have been at the top of the news for some time now; second, because we believe that one of the keys—perhaps *the* key—to reforming both programs is the adoption of the Fair-Tax. Remember, with the adoption of the FairTax, your Social Security and Medicare taxes disappear. These two programs will be funded out of general revenues—revenues supplied by the consumption tax. So, with your indulgence, we'll spend a few pages detailing the problems with Social Security and Medicare, and then tell you just how the FairTax can be the solution, or at least part of the solution.

America has always been a generous nation; we have always concerned ourselves with the problems of others as much as we have our own. That generous spirit, as it relates to Social Security and Medicare, is quickly driving both of these programs toward bankruptcy. We are facing a grave risk to the economic security of both the next generation of workers and the next generation of retirees.

It's time to test your knowledge on Social Security and Medicare. Here's a quick quiz:

1. Which program is expected to go bankrupt first: Social Security or Medicare?
2. How much of his or her paycheck does each American worker pay each month to support today's Social Security and Medicare programs?
3. How much do wealthy Americans living off their investment income and dividends pay each month to support Social Security and Medicare?
4. Do most working Americans pay more in income taxes or Social Security and Medicare taxes?

5. Myth or fact: Members of Congress and the president do not pay taxes to support Social Security and Medicare.
6. Myth or fact: Social Security is a retirement program that we all pay into and receive from proportionally—meaning that if one person retires after averaging $10,000 a year in earnings and another retires averaging $90,000 a year in earnings, the Social Security check received by the second retiree will be nine times that of the first retiree.

Now, here are the answers. Let's see how well you did.

1. Medicare. The Medicare Board of Trustees predicts that it will be bankrupt in 2020, while the Social Security Board of Trustees predicts that Social Security will not fail until 2041.
2. 7.65 percent . . . and the employer "pays" another 7.65 percent for each employee.[1]

---

1. Though it's not the subject of this book, something needs to be said about this idea that employers make a matching contribution to every worker's Social Security account in an amount equal to the Social Security tax withheld from the employee's paycheck. There is not one single serious and sober economist who is not working for the federal government who would support that fantasy. The so-called "matching contribution" paid by the employer is money taken from that sum budgeted by the employer to hire that worker. As such, it is, in reality, taken from the employee's earnings just as is the amount actually shown on the employee's check stub. However, for the purposes of this book, and to avoid introducing unnecessary controversy, we'll go along with the "matching contribution" nonsense.

3. Zero. Only those Americans who work for a living pay Social Security and Medicare taxes. Americans who receive millions and millions of dollars in income each year from stocks and bonds but don't receive a traditional "paycheck" never pay a penny in Social Security or Medicare taxes.

4. Most Americans (75 percent) pay more in Social Security and Medicare taxes than in income taxes.

5. Myth. Members of Congress and the president must have Social Security and Medicare taxes withheld from their paychecks just like every other American.

6. Myth. Social Security is an income redistribution and welfare program. Low-income Americans receive a check that replaces 90 percent of their preretirement income. Workers paying taxes on a $50,000 income will receive a check for only 32 percent of their preretirement income, and those workers paying taxes on $90,000 will receive a check covering just 15 percent of their preretirement income.

Social Security was enacted in the United States in 1935; the tax was first levied in 1937. Retirees first began receiving benefits the same year. In 1937 and 1938, the benefits were paid out in lump-sum form; it wasn't until 1939 that monthly benefits began. You won't be surprised to learn that there are good (if you want to use that word) stories about overpayments in both categories.

Originally the tax rate was 1 percent on the employee and 1 percent on the employer on the first $3,000 of "earned"

Fact Check: It's Unbelievable . . . But It's True

According to the Social Security Administration, the earliest reported Social Security benefit paid was a lump-sum benefit paid to a Cleveland man named Ernest Ackerman, who retired after paying into the Social Security system for one day. In that one day, he paid a nickel into Social Security. When he retired the following day, he qualified for a lump-sum payment of $0.17.

Such a system could never be sustained on the backs of young workers. Yet the real trouble started when monthly payments began for retirees. As an example, the first Social Security retirement check was issued to Ida May Fuller, a resident of Ludlow, Vermont. Ms. Fuller worked under and paid taxes into the Social Security system for three years before her retirement. In those three years, she paid a total of $24.75 in Social Security taxes, and yet her very first *monthly* check was $22.54. Over her lifetime, Ms. Fuller received a total of nearly $23,000 from monthly Social Security checks.

income. (There was no Social Security tax levied on "unearned" income such as dividends, asset sales, and capital gains.) Those paying the maximum paid $2.50 per month, and the employer matched it. The average contribution was about $1 per month per employee and employer. There were roughly forty-two workers paying retirement benefits for each retiree.

In 1965, Medicare was enacted; the tax was first levied in 1966. The rate was set at 0.35 percent on "earned" income for the employer and employee, and there was an earnings cap against which the tax could be levied, just as there is for Social Security. Again, as with Social Security, there was no tax levied on "unearned" income.

Over the ensuing years, the increasing costs caused the base wage against which the taxes were levied to be raised regularly. Both the Social Security wage base and tax rate has increased steadily over the years. The wage base today is $94,200, though there is pressure on Congress to increase it yet again. All of these increases mean that today, in 2006, every American worker and his employer will each pay 6.2 percent into Social Security on earnings up to $94,200 ($5,840 from the worker and $5,840 from his or her employer). An additional 2.9 percent combined from the worker and the employer will be paid into Medicare on 100 percent of our earnings.

Read that last line again closely. That's right: The Medicare tax is collected on 100 percent of your pay, no matter how much you earn. There is no longer a wage cap on Medicare taxes. You need to bear this in mind, because many in Washington think this is the best way to cure Social Security's cash flow ills. Just eliminate the wage cap and tax 100 percent of everyone's earnings!

While increasing taxes on those who make more than you might seem like a reasonable idea, doesn't eliminating all payroll taxes—including Social Security taxes—seem like a better plan?

Now, we know that the easiest way to empty a room when you want to be alone is to say, "Hey, let's talk about Social Security reform!" But try to bear with us a little longer here, because it's important to absorb a little more information in order to recognize the seriousness of the problem—and how the FairTax provides the ideal solution.

We now have slightly more than three workers paying for each retiree—and the baby boomers are about to retire. As the table on page 130 demonstrates, by the time our children retire, two of our grandchildren will have to share the burden of paying for each retiree's benefit.

There's one word to describe that table: *Catastrophe.*

How did this catastrophe happen? In large part, because the programs exploded in costs, forcing the increasing levies. Why? Because the simple fact is that when people receive a benefit they perceive as free, they never think it's enough. Social Security was devised during the Great Depression as a way to provide basic sustenance to those who had no money and no work to be able to survive. Today, however, that history is long forgotten, replaced with the almost universal view that Social Security is a sacred entitlement. This process was helped along by politicians, who eventually recognized that Social Security could provide a relatively handsome benefit for one class of voters—the elderly—while placing only a small burden on those still working. There were votes to be bought, so the political class dug in and got busy. Not only did benefits and taxes embark on a steady rise,

TABLE 13.1 Ratio of Social Security–Covered Workers to
Beneficiaries Calendar Years 1940–2075

Year	Covered Workers (in thousands)	Beneficiaries (in thousands)	Ratio
1940	35,390	222	159.4
1945	46,390	1,106	41.9
1950	48,280	2,930	16.5
1955	65,200	7,563	8.6
1960	72,530	14,262	5.1
1965	80,680	20,157	4.0
1970	93,090	25,186	3.7
1975	100,200	31,123	3.2
1980	113,656	35,118	3.2
1985	120,565	36,650	3.3
1990	133,672	39,470	3.4
1995	141,027	43,108	3.3
2000	154,732	45,166	3.4
2005	158,718	47,993	3.3
2010	166,717	52,604	3.2
2015	171,806	59,705	2.9
2020	176,049	67,977	2.6
2025	178,705	76,406	2.3
2030	181,110	83,524	2.2
2035	183,745	88,384	2.1
2040	186,581	91,077	2.0
2045	189,424	93,284	2.0
2050	191,869	95,340	2.0
2055	194,242	97,800	2.0
2060	196,467	100,389	2.0
2065	198,685	103,189	1.9
2070	200,774	105,828	1.9
2075	202,888	108,246	1.9

Source: 2005 Social Security Trustees Report.

they also added a disability benefit in 1956. An individual who has been categorized as "disabled" by doctors, under the definitions of the program, qualified for full Social Security benefits and Medicare regardless of age.

The hit on worker's paychecks remained generally small, but the political payoff to politicians grew steadily with each benefit increase.

The net result? We live in a country where it's hard not to know someone who is abusing this program. We've all heard the stories of someone who qualified for disability after an accident at work, but who now holds a new job where he works nights, gets paid in cash, and never declares a penny. Why isn't this kind of thing stopped? The political side of this writing team once actually tipped the Social Security Administration to someone who was working full time while collecting Social Security disability—only to be informed that they simply didn't have the workforce to look into the tens of thousands of similar reports. The lawyer-turned-talk-show-host can tell you of similar cases he encountered while representing clients seeking Social Security disability benefits. Actually, he won't—not just because of attorney-client privilege, but because he's a little embarrassed that he actually prevailed in some of those cases . . . and then got paid by the government to boot!

Medicare has seen its costs exploding in much the same way. When Lyndon Johnson gave his Great Society speech laying out his proposal for Medicare (for seniors) and Medicaid (for the poor) he claimed that by using readily available usage statistics we could project with some certainty that by

1990 Medicare would cost only $9 billion and Medicaid only $1 billion. He was a wee bit off. The actual cost of Medicare in 1990 was $110 billion; it has since risen to more than $300 billion.[2] By 1990, Medicaid costs had soared to $74 billion.[3] President Johnson must have been a terrible math student.

The simple fact is that politicians, unsurprisingly, don't seem to spend other folks' money as carefully as they spend their own. When it comes to government spending, the big three spending categories are Social Security, national defense, and Medicare.

The proposals for saving the retirement programs are many. Some politicians want to lift the earnings limit and levy the Social Security tax on 100 percent of our earnings. This, they believe, will "make the rich pay their fair share." Curiously, they also recommend lowering the levy on lower income earners. Having already essentially relieved the bottom 50 percent of income earners from any income tax liability at all, these politicians now want to work on payroll taxes. It's a sure way to earn voter loyalty, but a lousy way to reform the system.

President Bush, like many before him, has proposed allowing workers below a certain age to take a portion of their Social Security contribution and invest the money in one of a series of privately held packages of stocks

---

2. *Source:* 2004 Medicare Trustees Report.
3. What's worse? 1990 was a good year. Medicaid increased 27 percent annually over the next two years to reach $120 billion by 1992. *Source:* Urban Institute.

and/or bonds. These packages would require some certification or approval to prevent investors from being entirely speculative.

Over the long haul, it's clear that investments in the financial markets would produce far better retirement incomes than the current system. But that's over the long haul. How would Congress react to frequent market fluctuations, such as the one that occurred at the beginning of March 2001?

Here's how.

Members of the House and Senate, pandering to their constituents, would flock to the floors of their respective bodies and rail against the "ripoff artists on Wall Street that were manipulating the markets and destroying the retirement of the little people." This refrain would be sung by Democrats and Republicans alike (vote-buying, after all, is a bipartisan pastime). These deeply concerned (about their re-election) politicians would eagerly pass appropriations to take money from the general fund and replenish the funds they characterize as "stolen." Then they would rush home to their districts to hold press conferences and pat themselves on the back for saving the "little people."

Unfortunately, none of the proposed solutions—those above and others—can stabilize a system predicated on workers paying for retirees.

In the next twenty-five years, we will see a 100 percent increase in the number of American retirees. The number of workers, however, will increase by only 15 percent. Let's be realistic: Given those numbers, how can these programs survive? Under our current tax code, these programs can be maintained only by increasing the tax on those who work, reducing benefits for those who have retired, or by increasing the age of retirement. After all, in 1937 the average lifespan was 58 years.[4] Today it is 77.[5] Since 1940, the average lifespan remaining for those reaching 65 has increased by 25 percent for men and more than 30 percent for women as shown in the following table:

TABLE 13.2 Life Expectancy for Social Security

Year Cohort Turned 65	Percentage of Population Surviving from Ages 21 to 65		Average Remaining Life Expectancy for Those Surviving to Age 65	
	Male	Female	Male	Female
1940	53.9	60.6	12.7	14.7
1950	56.2	65.5	13.1	16.2
1960	60.1	71.3	13.2	17.4
1970	63.7	76.9	13.8	18.6
1980	67.8	80.9	14.6	19.1
1990	72.3	83.6	15.3	19.6

Source: http://www.ssa.gov/history/lifeexpect.html.

---

4. Life expectancy *at birth* in 1930 was 58 for men and 62 for women. However, the SSA makes a very persuasive case that only life expectancy after age 21 (thus eliminating infant mortality—infants who never paid into the SS system) is meaningful. That said, life expectancy after 21 has increased by over 20 years (though this actually adds Social Security revenues) since 1940 and life expectancy after 65 has increased by 3 years for men and 5 for women. *Source:* SSA; also Center for Disease Control and Prevention (CDC).
5. At birth, it is 77 years. Those who are 65 today (2002, actually) can expect to live to 83. *Source:* Center for Disease Control and Prevention (CDC).

Indeed, for all of the good intentions of those proposing "fixes," the system as it exists today is simply unsustainable. Dr. Larry Kotlikoff, chairman of the Economics Department at Boston University, recently concluded a study of Medicare and Social Security that showed that a permanent fix for Social Security and Medicare would cost $74 trillion in today's dollars. You heard me right: *Shortfall*—that is, money we don't have now and we sure won't have then. When you consider the fact that total household net wealth in this country—and that includes all of us—is only $43.8 trillion, you can see the problem.

(Let's pause for a moment and try to put the scale of a trillion-dollars into perspective. If you started a business on the day Jesus Christ was born and lost $1 million per day, through yesterday, it would take you another 734 years to lose $1 trillion. Now multiply that by 74, and you'll have a sense of how big the Social Security/Medicare shortfall really is.)

And just in case the problem hasn't quite come into focus for you, think about this: To cover the shortfall in Medicare and Social Security, the federal government would have to act *right now* to seize (confiscate, steal . . . however you care to phrase it) everything of value in every household in this nation—the equity in homes and cars, retirement funds, stocks and bonds, your cars, your socks, books, appliances, pet toys . . . everything—and apply the value of all those goodies against the shortfall in funding Social Security and Medicare. And even that would cover only about 60 percent of the funds that will be needed.

On second thought, seizing everything probably isn't that great an idea. Congress couldn't stand having all that money sitting around for the next seventy-five years. The politicians would immediately start borrowing from that stash to fund some new "urgently needed" vote-buying programs. There'd be a flurry of IOUs, and before you know it we'd be right back were we are today . . . in deep trouble.

Like they said in the movie: "Houston, we have a problem."

The only way to save those retirement programs, which are sacrosanct to the left—and the reason the left will ultimately climb on the FairTax bandwagon—is to change the way we collect the money needed to fund them. That's why the FairTax is so important to both Social Security and Medicare reform.

Here's the difference: The FairTax will raise money from the overall size of the economy, not just from Americans currently working. Since the FairTax applies to every retail purchase, this means that 300 million Americans—plus about 50 million visitors to our shores—will be adding to federal revenues every time they make a purchase.

Economists have made some amazing predictions as to how our economy would grow with the FairTax. If, as many predict, we double the size of our economy in the first fifteen years after passage of the FairTax, we will also double the federal revenues from which Social Security and Medicare must be paid.

Passage of the FairTax will also essentially eliminate the cap on revenue collections for Social Security and Medicare. Today, as we've noted, there is a cap on earnings subject to the levy for Social Security. Medicare taxes are levied against all "earned" income. Workers earning at or below the cap pay on every dollar of income. Do the rich pay Social Security taxes on every dollar of their income? Hardly. Nor do they pay Medicare taxes on every dollar of income, for that matter—sure, technically there is no cap when it comes to Medicare, but the rich have the resources to manipulate and control just how they receive their income. The regular wage earner cannot.

Let's take just one quick example of how the wealthy can limit their tax liability—including their liability to pay Medicare and Social Security taxes. We can pick on lawyers (after all, it's a cherished national pastime).

Our sample lawyer sues doctors and drug companies. He gets multimillion-dollar awards for his clients, and in turn he collects millions in compensation for his hard work, sweat, and tears. Now, does the lawyer pay Medicare taxes on his entire share of the jury's award? Hardly. Our lawyer, you see, has protected himself by setting up a limited liability corporation or a professional corporation. The check goes to the corporation, which then pays a salary to the lawyer, from which Social Security and Medicare taxes are withheld. What about the rest of the money, you ask? Have you ever heard of corporate dividends? Did you know you don't pay Social Security or Medicare taxes on dividends?

Just how would things be different under the FairTax? Let's go back to the lawyer. Under the FairTax, it wouldn't really matter how the lawyer earned his wealth, be it salary or dividend income. It would matter how he spent it. When he takes $1.5 million from his wealth portfolio and spends it on a gleaming new yacht or airplane, he pays the FairTax, no matter how that money was earned. The FairTax, you see, is a way to bring people of great wealth, but minimal income, into the taxpaying fold—to get their help in supporting the retirement benefit programs that will end up being the principal means of retirement support for 90 million people in the next twenty years.

Another advantage? The FairTax would give the average income worker a 50 percent increase in take-home pay. Money that is invested is not taxed. Americans will invest as never before. In fact, after the FairTax is implemented, capital investment will increase quickly by a staggering 76 percent. As Americans become an investor class of unprecedented proportion, they will find themselves less dependent on Social Security for their retirement income.

The best way to reform Social Security, after all, might be to bring about an aging population that doesn't need it.

14

INCOME TAX OUTRAGES

As you can tell by now, one reason the FairTax Plan has proven attractive to so many Americans is that it means getting rid of our current tax system—including the Internal Revenue Service.

Since the IRS is nobody's idea of a cherished public service, we thought a chapter on IRS outrages might shine another useful light on the promise of the FairTax revolution. This chapter serves two purposes. First, it will give you, the reader, the chance to utter phrases like "Poor guy," or "What a gang of crooks and idiots!" It also gives you an opportunity to reflect on what the world will be like when a truly voluntary tax system (the FairTax comes to mind) comes along, making outrages like these nothing more than historical anecdotes . . . unless, of course, they happened to you.

Americans have learned, often the hard way, of the terrible consequences that can flow from not following closely the letter of the law—a law that many IRS employees themselves can't even evaluate or quote accurately. We could easily fill several volumes with stories of IRS actions against taxpayers, but we'll hold it to just a few.

On March 22, 1985, the Associated Press sent a story down the wires headlined "IRS Tries to Penalize Chemical Company $46,000 for Being a Dime Short." The so-called offender here was Rohm & Haas of Philadelphia, a company that makes chemicals that do everything from keeping fruits fresh to fighting disease. They also own the Morton salt brand. Rohm & Haas is a large enough company that in 1983 they sent a check to the IRS, in payment of payroll taxes, in the amount of $4,448,112.88. They actually owed $4,448,112.98. The check was exactly ten cents short. So . . . did the IRS call and ask for their dime like any reasonable businessman would have done? Are you kidding? This is the IRS we're talking about here. It's penalty time! The IRS sent Rohm & Haas a letter telling them that they now owed $46,806.37 in penalties . . . all for being one dime short on the remittance of payroll taxes. It took many months, and no small amount spent on legal fees, to get the IRS to drop the penalty. (We believe that the IRS eventually got their dime.)

That's a comical story, but sometimes the arrogance of the IRS can lead to genuine tragedy. The story of Alex and Kay Council shows the tragic lengths to which an honest citizen can be driven by IRS enforcement actions. In the late 1970s, an insurance executive named Alex Council received a sizable bonus at work and got involved in a tax shelter. His tax accountant told him it was a legitimate option, but the IRS disagreed. Council's liability for taxes due on the bonus expired at the end of three years. Nonetheless, after the statute of limitations had expired, the IRS sent the Councils a notice demanding more than $180,000 in unpaid taxes on the bonus, a figure including penalties and interest. The Councils' accountant notified the IRS that the statute of limitations had expired on the Councils' tax liability. Two years later, the IRS wrote back to claim that they had mailed a certified letter to the Councils prior to the expiration of the statute notifying them of the deficiency. Okay, fair enough—show us a copy of the certified letter and the receipt! No way. Not only did the IRS refuse to provide copies and a receipt for the letter, they wouldn't even tell the Councils where the letter had been sent until yet another two years had passed. Well, wouldn't you know it—when the IRS finally coughed up the address to which they supposedly had sent the delinquency notice. You guessed it. Wrong address!

Now, you'd think this would pretty much be the end of things, wouldn't you? By virtue of sending the notice to the wrong address, the IRS had failed to inform the Councils of their tax liability within the time allotted. Well, that's not the way the IRS operates. When this matter found its way into the federal court system, the IRS informed the court that it was the Councils' responsibility to prove they *hadn't* received the notice. In other words, the Councils had to undertake the impossible task of proving a negative. Apparently the old innocent-until-proven-guilty idea never really caught on with the tax collector.

As you might guess, the Councils couldn't prove they didn't receive the notice, so the IRS slapped a lien on their construction business for almost $300,000. The lien destroyed Alex Council's credit rating, and his business collapsed. Shortly thereafter, Alex Council left his wife the following letter:

My dearest Kay,

I have taken my life in order to provide capital for you. The IRS and its liens which have been taken against our property illegally by a runaway agency of our government have dried up all sources of credit for us. So I have made the only decision I can. It's purely a business decision. I hope you can understand that. I love you completely.

Alex

PS: You will find my body on the north side of the house.

Ultimately, the court threw out the IRS's claim against the Councils. But that was too late to save Alex's life.

You can even run afoul of the IRS by just trying to do something nice for someone else. Professional golfer Lee Trevino once had a caddy who was in need of open heart surgery, but he had no health insurance. Lee Trevino generously offered to cover the cost of the surgery—but that didn't sit too well with the IRS. They wanted their ounce of flesh, too. Not only did Trevino cover the cost of his caddy's surgery, he had to write a check to the IRS in payment of a gift tax to boot! Just another entry into the list of examples that no good deed goes unpunished.

Perhaps you're wondering whether we, your humble authors, have any personal experiences of mistreatment from the IRS. The coauthor who is an elected representative of the people, as it turns out, happens to be squeaky clean when it comes to tax matters; he could think of nothing that might interest the reader. The coauthor who is an attorney and talk show host, on the other hand, labors under no such limitations. So here, in his words, is the story of yet another IRS outrage.

It was in the mid-1980s. My accountant surprised me with the news that I owed the IRS about $50,000 with the filing of my tax return. That was $50,000 I didn't have. I knew that not filing was a crime, so I filed without paying the $50,000—and then immediately contacted the IRS and asked to speak to an agent. I told him of my situation, and he agreed to work with me over the period of a year to cover the remainder of my tax liability.

Several months later, I settled a rather large case on which I was paid a contingency fee large enough to allow me to satisfy my outstanding balance with the IRS.

I called the local IRS office to speak to the agent who had been working with me. Another agent came on the line to tell me that the agent with whom I had been working had been reassigned, and that she would be handling my case instead. The conversation went like this:

"Mr. Smith has been working with me on my past due taxes," I began. "I have the money to pay the entire balance due right now, and I need to know what the total is."

"Well, Mr. Boortz, why haven't you paid your taxes before now?"

"Because I didn't have the money."

"Couldn't you have borrowed the money?"

"Excuse me, ma'am. Does it really matter why I haven't paid? I have the money now, and I want to go to the bank, get a cashier's check, and run it over to you right now. Today. This afternoon. All I need is to know what I owe."

"Well, I want to know why you haven't paid before now."

"Like I told you, I didn't have the money."

"Well, you could have sold something to pay your taxes."

"This is rather ridiculous, isn't it? Here I am, asking you for a figure so that I can bring certified funds over right now, and you won't give it to me. Don't you have a legal obligation to tell a taxpayer how much money he owes when he requests the information?"

"I'll get back to you."

With that, the lovely Sandra[1] hung up. I waited for her to call back with a figure, but never heard back. I made a note to call her back the next morning and headed home.

Early the next morning, my secretary rushed into my office to tell me that the lobby was full of IRS agents demanding to see me. I walked into my lobby to see the lovely Sandra accompanied by three gun-toting special agents. When I invited them back to my office, Sandra stepped up to my desk and slapped a notice of seizure down in front of me. "We're seizing your office building due to your failure to pay your income taxes." She turned on her heel, let it run for a while,

---

1. Yes, Sandra. And I remember her last name too. Some people you never forget.

and turned it off.[2] Then she stomped out of the office. The armed agents looked embarrassed. One of them actually winked at me and shrugged his shoulders. The entire matter was settled in hours: I finally got the payoff figure, delivered the certified funds, and the seizure was canceled.

So why did our friend Sandra refuse to give me the payoff figure over the phone? Why did she serve me with a notice of seizure the next morning? Simple: to make herself look good in the eyes of her superiors. Sandra would gain no particular glory with her supervisors by simply quoting a payoff figure over the phone and accepting a check. It would be far more impressive to go to her superiors and tell them something like: "Yeah, so I'm going through the files and I find this Neal Boortz guy. He owes more than fifty thousand dollars, and nobody's even filed a lien! So I slap a seizure notice on his office building, and wouldn't you know it—he's over here with a check in three hours!" We're told that on occasion IRS agents get a bonus for a collection following a seizure. Not a bad little racket.

We could go on for hours detailing abuses that have happened at the hands of the IRS,[3] but our goal in this book is to promote the FairTax, not run down the IRS. The point of mentioning these incidents of taxpayers being abused by the federal government is that *they simply wouldn't happen* under

---

2. Okay. I know that's an old Steve Allen line. I just couldn't resist. N.B.
3. An excellent source for stories of IRS outrages is James Bovard's bestseller, *Lost Rights: The Destruction of American Liberty* (St. Martin's Press, 1994).

the FairTax. Rohm & Hass would have had no payroll taxes to pay, and thus no $47,000 fine for being a dime short. Alex Council could have enjoyed his bonus without searching for a tax shelter; he would have paid his taxes when he spent his money and would have been able to live out his years in contentment with his wife and family.

As for your humble coauthor? Well, he would have found another way to upset the system, no matter what the system was. But that's neither here nor there.

15

QUESTIONS
AND OBJECTIONS

We've been working together on this FairTax idea for
so long that we know just about every nuance of the
system—and every conceivable objection to the proposal—
like the back of our collective hands. So we thought it would
be useful to go through our huge file of letters, e-mails, and
notes taken during FairTax discussions on the radio, during
town hall meetings, and in other public forums, and take up
a number of questions and objections regarding the idea of a
national retail sales tax. Undoubtedly you will come up with
questions we haven't answered in this book. Well, that's
what e-mail and talk shows are for.

For now, let's start with these:

How was the 23 percent FairTax rate decided?

For this, we go back to that group of Houston businessmen who first sat down to try to find a fair, reasonable, and efficient way to overhaul our tax system. After they settled on the idea of a national consumption tax, they sought expert opinions on how much that tax must be in order to duplicate the revenue the federal government would have received from the various taxes eliminated by the FairTax. The researchers and analysts concluded that we would need an inclusive sales tax rate of 23 percent. A number of studies designed to verify and refine that figure are currently under way. Some recent results suggest that with our growing economy, and with new estimates of additional economic growth under the FairTax Plan, the final inclusive tax rate could be a percentage point or two less. The end rate will be determined by Congress when the FairTax is implemented.

But I've heard critics say the tax would have to be higher—much higher.

Those critics are responding to their own distorted version of the FairTax Plan—a version that's calculated to alarm listeners about the implications of the Plan. For instance, these critics ignore the fact that, under this system, the federal government itself would be a major taxpayer: All sales at the retail level, whether to individuals or the government, will carry the tax. These critics also conclude that the K Street lobbyists will be successful at manipulating their contacts in Congress to gain certain exemptions and exclusions. When you stick with the parameters outlined in the FairTax legislation, these higher figures are wild exaggerations.

Will the FairTax be increased over time? Decreased?

The FairTax rate was set at a flat 23 percent because that's the rate required to maintain the same level of tax revenue currently collected by the government. The authors and supporters of the FairTax certainly hope, and expect, that the rate will go down in the future. Some of our nation's preeminent economists predict incredible growth in the American economy once the FairTax is enacted. If Congress can keep government spending down, that strong economic growth should bring the FairTax down as well.

For the moment, though, let's address the actual wording in H.R. 25. The FairTax bill includes a formula for setting the rate in future years. That formula is included in the bill for one simple reason: to ensure that the Social Security and Medicare trust funds are at least as well funded tomorrow as they are today. The goal is to keep any detractors from challenging the FairTax as a ploy to destroy or weaken Social Security or Medicare. As long as the present funding levels for Social Security are maintained, those charges won't stick.

Do we want to do more and actually restructure Social Security and Medicare so that they can be viable in the future? Absolutely. Do we want to reduce government spending on wasteful programs, thus saving money and allowing us to lower the rate? Absolutely. But we think you'll agree that repealing the tax code and replacing it with the FairTax is already a lofty goal. Cutting government spending, saving

Medicare and Social Security, and pulling out the income tax by its roots all at the same time might be a little ambitious, don't you think? We thought so—and that's why the rate looks the way it does.

In sum, the FairTax rate—and the adjustment formula included in the bill—are a way of saying to the American people, "Let's abolish this crazy and punishing income tax code, and this regressive payroll tax, and replace them both with a simple consumption tax. All the other arguments can wait for another day." As we see it, the first job is to elect some congressmen and senators who will support the FairTax. It needs to be said, however, that even after the FairTax is implemented, voters must never drop their guard. Even if the federal government's revenue collection machine is revolutionized, it doesn't mean the political thirst for our money will abate. If voters stop worrying about where their money's going, politicians will look for a way to raise the rate or find new sources of revenue. Whoever said that eternal vigilance is the price of liberty had it just about nailed.[1]

So when I go to the store to buy a $100 coat, will I now have to pay $123?

The short answer is, No. The longer answer is also No, but it depends on what exactly you mean by the question.

If you're asking whether a $100 coat you see for sale *before* passage of the FairTax Plan will cost $123 under the Plan,

---

1. It was Wendell Phillips speaking before the Massachusetts Antislavery Society in 1852.

the answer is no, because—as you'll remember from previous chapters—that $100 price is already inflated by 22 percent worth of embedded tax. Once those embedded taxes fall away, the 23 percent FairTax will bring the price right back to the $100 level.

If you're asking whether a $100 coat you see for sale *after* passage of the FairTax will actually set you back $123, the answer is no because the FairTax was designed as what's called an "inclusive" tax—that is, the tax is included in the list price of the product. When you go to the store and purchase an item for $100, in other words, the retailer will get $77; the remaining $23 is paid to the federal government. This is the biggest difference between the FairTax and most current state sales taxes, which are "exclusive"—that is, added to the price of the merchandise at the time of the sale. Since our current income taxes are figured on an inclusive basis—that is, they are taken out of our paychecks, not added to them—it was decided to handle the sales tax in exactly the same manner.

I've read some critical articles claiming that the sales tax will really be 30 percent or more, not 23 percent. Who's telling the truth?

In a sense, both sides are. But critics of the FairTax have a way of dwelling on this 30 percent figure, so we're going to spend some time on the answer to this question. Let's see if we can make it interesting as well.

What's at issue here is the mathematical equivalent of a game of semantics. And the crux of the matter is the distinction between inclusive and exclusive taxes that we just mentioned.

Right now, almost all federal taxes are figured on an inclusive basis. The prime example would be your federal income tax. To calculate the amount of federal income tax you owe, you multiply your taxable income by your effective tax rate, subtract that amount and send it to the government. A married couple reporting $112,000 in taxable income, for example, would fall into the 25 percent tax bracket. Because 25 percent of $112,000 is $28,000,[2] that's how much the couple would owe in federal income tax.

But there's another way to figure your tax rate—the tax exclusive way. Here's how it works: After paying their $28,000, this couple would have $84,000 in their bank account. Here's how the critics get their 30-plus percent number: They look at $28,000 *as a percentage of the $84,000*, not of the original $112,000. An exclusive rate will always be higher than its corresponding inclusive rate. Our highest income tax bracket is 35 percent. Expressed as an exclusive rate, this would be closer to 54 percent. In both cases, the revenue collected is exactly the same. The only thing that changes is the rhetoric.

Now let's apply these definitions to sales tax rates. Let's say that, after the FairTax is passed, you set your sights on a $100 toaster. (Okay, it's a pretty nice toaster.) When you pick up that little beauty at the store, the retailer sends $23 to the federal government as sales tax and keeps $77. The government gets 23 percent of your purchase price. The sales

---

2. With the graduated income tax rates, this figure would actually be closer to $21,475. For this example, we'll ignore the graduated rates in order to keep this explanation reasonably understandable.

tax was included—it was an "inclusive" sales tax. If, on the other hand, you walked into a retailer working on a tax-exclusive basis and bought that same toaster for $77, and he added $23 in sales tax for a total price of $100, the sales tax rate would be 29.9 percent. There's the 30 percent critics are quoting. In each case, you pay exactly the same for the item, and exactly the same dollar amount in sales tax. The only difference is in how you figure the rate: As an inclusive tax it's 23 percent, as an exclusive tax it's 30 percent.

Let's reduce this entire discussion down to one question. Do you think the opponents of the FairTax would rather have you believe you'll be paying 23 cents worth of sales tax out of every dollar you spend, or 30 cents? That's a real toughie, isn't it?

They never miss a trick.

Isn't the FairTax really just a VAT tax like they have in Europe?

All right, we've been over this already. But it's a sore point, so we'll answer again:

No! Absolutely not! Bite your tongue!

"VAT" stands for value-added tax. The VAT is essentially a sales tax that is added *at every step in the production of retail goods*. The VAT is popular with politicians, for the very reason that the people should shun it: It's capable of producing huge amounts of revenue while remaining virtually hidden from consumers. When a consumer pays for a product in a country that has instituted a VAT system, he has no real idea how much tax he is paying to the federal government. That, of course, is an ideal situation for politicians, since it's hard to resent a tax that remains invisible to the naked eye—but of course it's a terrible situation for consumers. Since the tax is so well hidden in the long line of companies involved in the manufacturing and merchandising process, it can easily be increased without undue public scrutiny. When VAT rates are increased, it looks just like another increment of inflation to the unaware consumer. Nobel Prize–winning economist Milton Friedman said it best: "The VAT is the most efficient way to raise revenue for the government. It is also the most effective way to increase the size of government."

It's central to the design of the FairTax that it is added *only once:* at the point of sale to the retail purchaser. It's an upfront charge, not a series of hidden costs. The consumer is completely aware of what he is paying and will be aware of any political attempts to increase the rate. If you hear someone refer to the FairTax as a VAT, you can be sure you're listening to someone who hasn't done his homework . . . or who, for whatever reason, is trying to torpedo the FairTax.

Some politicians have suggested to combine the income tax and the VAT. Wouldn't that be a better idea?

Yeah. That would be a great idea—for politicians, not taxpayers. A combination VAT and income tax would give you the worst elements of both. The huge compliance costs and invasions of your financial privacy that come with an income tax would still be in place, as would the IRS. The payroll taxes would stay in place, along with all the business and corporate taxes that flow into the system today. Yet on top of all this would be the increase in consumer prices a VAT automatically generates.

There . . . aren't you ashamed for even *asking* that question?

You say the FairTax will also replace the alternative minimum tax. What's that all about?

Glad you asked, because if this tax monster isn't put out of our misery—and soon—it is going to nail more and more hard-working Americans as the years go by.

The alternative minimum tax (AMT) was introduced in 1969 as a "spite" tax. It seems that some politicians didn't like the fact that just a few years earlier 150,000 high-achieving individuals rudely took advantage of the perfectly legal deductions and credits available to them—and paid no federal income tax. WHOA! Can't let *that* happen. Everybody's gotta pay taxes, even when the law says you don't owe any! (Unless, of course, you're poor.) So the alternative minimum tax was passed to force a second calculation of your earnings and deductions. How does it work? If a taxpayer's deductions exceed a certain percentage of their gross income, they lose deductions. That'll teach 'em!

The bad news? The AMT was never indexed to inflation—a little fact that eluded the average American during the debate on the AMT legislation, since most American taxpayers were completely uninterested in the proceedings. After all, wasn't this just a way to go after fat cats? The prevailing attitude toward taxes in this country still follows former Senator

Russell Long's saying: "Don't tax him. Don't tax me. Tax that man behind the tree." (It was that same mindset that brought us the Sixteenth Amendment in the first place.)

Today, however, thanks to the failure to index the AMT to inflation, disaster is waiting around the corner. By 2010, about 35 million Americans will be forced to pay the AMT. The victims will no longer be just "high-earning individuals," but middle Americans.

For some time now, Democrats and Republicans alike have been trying to find a way to abolish the AMT. They know, and wisely fear, the reaction they will face when their middle-income constituents discover that they are "fat cats." Unfortunately, the elimination of the AMT will cost about $700 billion in revenues over ten years. In fact—and you might want to sit down before you read this—at the rate we're going, by 2010 or so it will cost the country less (in terms of lost revenue) to jettison the income tax than it would to get rid of the AMT.

The FairTax solves that problem overnight.

If this is such a great idea, why hasn't it been tried elsewhere?

Well, here's something else that no other foreign government has ever tried: relying exclusively on an income and payroll tax for funding essential government operations. We are not a country that waits for others to try and perfect something before we'll give it a try. In fact, the world's tenth and fifteenth largest economies do pretty much what we are proposing. (What are those economies, you ask? Spain? Italy? Nope—Texas and Florida.) The United States has always been a world leader . . . so let's not be afraid to lead here as well.

Instead of offering a (p)rebate, why not just exempt certain items like food and medicine?

Early on, it was clearly understood that the American people would reject any idea for tax reform if that idea put an additional burden of taxation on our nation's low and middle-income families. The idea of a national retail sales tax wouldn't get into the ballpark, let alone to first base, if it involved requiring our poor families to give up 23 cents out of every dollar they spend. This is why the prebate was created: to ensure that *nobody* in America—from the very poor to the very rich—would end up paying a sales tax on the basic necessities of life. So, why not just exempt those basic necessities from the FairTax?

Studies have shown that high-income earners spend proportionately more on items that might be described as basic necessities, like food and clothing. Would it be fair to allow a multimillionaire to spend $20,000 on food for a large wedding reception at his estate, and not pay any sales tax on that purchase? If you try to put controls in place that would bring the sales tax into play when spending reached a certain limit, you would be adding a completely unnecessary level of bureaucracy and regulation that could easily be circumvented by a clever party-giver.

By the same token, exempting certain items—such as food and prescription drugs—would again open the door to an entire battalion of lobbyists to argue that the portion of the industry that they represent is clearly an essential product. Health care would come first. Then food, prescription drugs, real estate . . . see where this is going? Half of the economy would soon be exempted as "essential," and that half without the money to hire lobbyists would pay for the government with a tax rate in the 50 percent range.

The simplest solution is to ensure, through the prebate mechanism, that nobody pays sales taxes on spending up to the poverty level. Poverty-level spending is, by definition, that spending necessary for a household of a given size to pay for its necessities. It is adjusted every year by the Department of Health and Human Services. This system will actually work out better for many families: Households that grow a portion of their own food or sew their own clothes or buy used goods, for example, will be able to bank some of their monthly rebate payment, or spend that money on items not considered necessities!

Clearly, the monthly prebate is the best solution for all . . . and by far the easiest to implement.

What about state or local sales taxes and state payroll taxes?

The FairTax affects only federal taxes. It's up to the various states to reform and modify their own tax systems, if that's what they believe their citizens want.

Having said that, after the implementation of the FairTax, we expect that the state governments will start feeling tremendous pressure to conform their own tax systems to the national FairTax system. The end result? Many, if not all, states will likely bow to political pressure and remove all income, payroll, corporate, and business taxes, and subscribe to the same inclusive sales tax used by the federal government.

The governors we have talked with say they'd be very likely to eliminate state income taxes, since each state that levies an income tax uses federal regulations to determine taxable income—regulations that would now be obsolete. They also say they would welcome a move to taxing all goods and services with no exclusions or exemptions. Why? Not only would such a system be easier to administer, but it would also broaden the tax base (with the addition of taxes on services). Eliminating exclusions and exemptions would also allow the states to reduce their tax rate dramatically. One study of the revenue of one of our larger states—one with no income tax and a sales tax on goods that varies from 7.75 percent to 8.25 percent—showed that moving to a tax on all goods and services, with no exclusions or exemptions, would allow the state to reduce its tax rate to 2.5 percent without losing a dime in revenue.

And there's another giant reason to opt for a sales tax with no exemptions: In 2003, the states lost more than $23 billion in collections from Internet and catalog sales—a figure that's only going to explode in the coming years. The FairTax will recapture that income.

What if I buy a used car?

Used car, used home—it doesn't matter: The FairTax will only apply to the sale of *new* consumer goods purchased at the retail level—not to used items. No citizen will be burdened with the responsibility of having to collect sales taxes on the sale of their personal property, be it homes, cars, boats, or anything else. Title II A, Section 201, 1(2) of the FairTax Act says that the purpose of the FairTax is "to tax all consumption of goods and services in the United States once, without exception, but only once." Once the tax is paid on a car, home, blender, or any other consumer good or service, that's it.

Will there be a sales tax on the next home I buy?

If you purchase that home new, from a developer or home builder, yes, the 23 percent FairTax will be included in the sales price. But despair not! Economists have estimated the embedded taxes on new home construction to be about 25 percent. The new home market is extremely competitive, and once these embedded taxes are removed, the price of new homes will drop immediately. In the final analysis, a new home, complete with the inclusive FairTax, may cost less than that home would have cost under our current tax structure.

Again, remember that under the new system you'll be getting 100 percent of your paycheck. If you're making $60,000 per year, instead of taking home around $3,800 per month to pay your mortgage and living expenses (as you are now), under the FairTax you'll take home $5,000 per month. Interest rates will decline by about 30 percent, so your payments will be lower, while the money you save and invest won't be taxed. You'll be getting that sales tax rebate check or credit every month, and still go out and buy a new home for no more than you would pay without the FairTax—and quite possibly less!

Whoa! Hold on a minute. What about my home mortgage interest deduction?

Real estate agents say, "If we can't calculate a mortgage interest deduction, we'll sell fewer homes." To which we offer the obvious answer: "If you think interest deductions sell homes, try doubling the interest rate. Do you expect to sell twice as many homes?" Of course not. In fact, real estate agents calculate interest deductions because it's a quick and easy way of showing the buyer how much more take-home pay they'll have to pay their mortgage. And after all of the calculating is done, 65 percent of taxpayers file a short form with standard deductions and do not deduct the mortgage interest anyway!

It's simple: The home mortgage interest deduction only has value if there's an income tax. It's a *deduction*, after all—a deduction from a tax that, under the FairTax Plan, you'd no longer be paying. To put it another way, mortgage interest deductions scrape a bit off the top of your income taxes, but the FairTax eliminates them altogether. Which option do you prefer?

Of course, the real estate industry's lobbying firms in Washington will be virulent opponents of the FairTax. They simply won't relent in their pressure to prevent any taxes on the sale of a new home. The only thing they miss is that the taxes in place *now* are far bigger, and more likely to impede new home sales, than the FairTax Plan.

I've wanted my own home for years. Will the FairTax help that dream come true?

If you're saving for the down payment on a home now, you're saving after-tax dollars. Depending on your tax bracket, you might have to earn as much as $1,000 just to have $500 to put toward your dream home. Under the FairTax Plan, you'll be saving for your new home with untaxed dollars. You'll only have to earn $500 to save $500. Remember, you're taxed only when you spend. That money you're putting aside for your future plans will not be taxed. Also, remember: Mortgage companies are just as subject to embedded taxes as any other retailer or service provider! Once lenders start operating without tax consequences, you'll see a drop in interest rates. Like retail goods, new homes won't be any more expensive, even with the FairTax added. Furthermore, interest rates will be cheaper, and you'll be saving money faster. With the FairTax, you'll be in your own home a lot sooner than you might think—and you might even have enough money left over to pay for a nice spa, where you can relax with a glass of your favorite adult beverage every April 15.

If the price of a new home is reduced by over 20 percent because all embedded taxes are removed, what's that going to do to the value of the home I already own?

Nothing. Yes, the price of new homes will go down after the implementation of the FairTax. That reduction in price will be offset by the FairTax itself, the end result being that people will be paying pretty much the same price for these homes after as before the FairTax. Your advantage is that when you sell your home there will be no sales tax—because your home is used, remember? The FairTax applies only to the sale of new consumer items. So you'll still be competing on a level playing field with the developers.

Is it really necessary to tax services, too? Can't we just stick to taxing the items we buy?

Not too long ago, the FairTax was being explained to a group of physicians in Washington, D.C. Five minutes into the presentation, they were cheering the idea. After about ten minutes, though, one physician suddenly realized that the tax would be levied against all goods *and services*.

She raised her hand in alarm. "You're not going to ask doctors to collect taxes from their patients, are you?"

"Of course," the speaker responded. "What makes you think you're so special?"

Okay, maybe that was a little flippant, but the point stands. Government ought to be neutral . . . period. We should not be in the business of picking winners and losers. Most physicians, dentists, and lawyers make good livings from their patients and clients. As they earn these livings, they're relieved of the burden of helping to collect the revenues to run the government while their neighbors are forced to do so.

Indeed, the embedded cost of the IRS for medical services is about 26 percent. They are collecting this tax now—they just don't know it.

Won't churches and charities suffer if charitable giving is not deductible?

In a word: No! Americans don't give to charities for tax deductions. They give to charities because they want to be helpful. Indeed, some of the great fortunes that have been given away (by names like Gould, Frick, Mellon, and Carnegie) were given away before the income tax, and thus deductibility, were even enacted.

These ideas are not new. The eighteenth-century philosopher and economist Adam Smith wrote that man's nature "interest[s] him in the fortunes of others, and render[s] their happiness necessary to him, though he derive[s] nothing from it except the pleasure of seeing it."

In 1980, the top marginal tax rate was 70 percent. That means that every dollar at the margin that was contributed to charity reduced the donor's taxes by 70 cents. Just 30 cents came out of his pocket. We gave $40 billion to charities that year. By 1988, we had dramatically reduced the top marginal tax to 28 percent, thus reducing the value of charitable contributions. We gave nearly $200 billion to charities that year. *Money* magazine reports that the average American donates $1,600 annually, even though two-thirds of all Americans receive no tax deduction because they don't itemize those contributions on their tax returns.

Finally, more than 70 percent of the money that goes to nonprofit groups comes from businesses they run. The Red Cross sells blood. Your university sells you mugs and hats. The Girl Scouts sell you cookies. And remember, 65 percent of us do not deduct, yet we still give to the church.

Let's make it just this simple: How many people do you know who give money simply to get a tax deduction? With taxes at the 35 percent level, why would they spend $1,000 to save $350?

How will the switch to the FairTax be made?

Cold turkey!

On January 1, we'll begin to get our gross pay with no deductions. We'll also begin to see a sales tax at the retail level. Businesses will use the thousands of employees whose job has been to minimize taxes for more productive pursuits.

The plan's one "transition rule," which we mentioned earlier, says that the value of any inventory on hand on December 31 can be used as a credit against collecting taxes in the next year. So a tire distributor with $1 million in tires on hand on December 31, for example, can bank the first million dollars of sales in the next year without collecting the tax, because the tax has already been collected on the manufacture of those tires and has been paid.

Some will argue that such a rule would "cost" the government income. We repeat: The tax on those goods has already been collected, and then embedded in the cost of that inventory of tires. There will be, we admit, a delay in collections. At any given time, there's about $1.2 to $1.4 trillion in business inventories in America. Not collecting the tax on that inventory will slow collections by about $350 billion. Still, compare that to the trillions we must come up with to solve the Social Security and Medicare crisis.

And remember, this plan solves the Social Security and Medicare problems, too!

What if politicians just keep raising the FairTax rate?

That will be your fault.

Yes, sad to say, the FairTax won't absolve you of your responsibilities as a U.S. citizen. If you keep electing people who will raise your taxes, shame on you. The FairTax Act changes the way revenues are raised for the legitimate operations of the federal government of the United States. It's a tax reform measure, not a government reform measure. Passing the FairTax Act doesn't allow you to drop your guard when it comes to monitoring the actions of your elected representatives in Washington. Could your senators and representatives increase the FairTax rate? Yes, they could, just as they can (and have) increased the income tax rates. What they will lose, however, is the ability to raise the sales tax rate on just one segment of the population (the rich), while trying to curry favor with another segment (the not-rich).

In the final analysis, you must continue to be an informed and involved citizen—and when election time comes around, you must let your candidates know you're paying attention.

How will the FairTax create jobs?

Simple—through economic expansion. As we've said, economists estimate that the economy can be expected to grow at a rate of more than 10 percent in the first year after the adoption of the FairTax. Businesses will need new workers to keep up with the needs of a quickly growing economy.

Consider what we're facing today: Jobs are moving offshore because the 22 percent embedded cost of the IRS in the price system makes us less competitive in the global economy. Businesses are moving offshore so that they can manufacture their products in a nation with a less punishing tax burden, so that they can lower their prices to be more competitive. As we mentioned earlier, nations with a VAT rebate the VAT upon exporting their goods overseas. They still have some tax component in their price system, but much less than we do. If we succeed in getting all taxes out of our price system—by eliminating all business and payroll taxes and compliance costs—no foreign corporation will be able to compete with us. In order to be competitive, every foreign multinational corporation will build its next plant in the United States so that it can compete with us in a global economy.

If there are no more payroll taxes, how will the government fund Social Security?

The FairTax is no more a Social Security reform measure than it is a government reform measure. As we've noted, the Fair-Tax rate is set to be revenue neutral: the federal government will be taking in as much revenue under the FairTax as it now takes in with the income tax, payroll taxes, the death tax, capital gains taxes, and the rest of the government levies you've come to know and love. So don't worry: *The money will be there to fund Social Security.* (It should be pointed out that the present Social Security receives funding only from the Social Security payroll tax.)

Under the FairTax Plan, the number of people paying into the system will grow from about 159 million workers to 300 million Americans—and about 50 million visitors to our shores. That's right: Even visitors to America from abroad will be, in effect, paying into the Social Security system through their retail purchases. In addition, the FairTax removes the earnings limit on what income will be subject to Social Security taxes. Under our proposal, *every* penny spent will contribute to our retirement programs. So, although the FairTax isn't a Social Security reform measure, it will relieve the urgent need for such reform, so that our politicians can (we hope) do something constructive in that regard.

Will there still be records on how much I paid into the Social Security System?

Yes, your employer will still submit records of the number of quarters during which you are gainfully employed. Those records will be used to determine your Social Security eligibility.

Shouldn't we work on reforming Social Security first?

Since we're talking about Social Security and Medicare, we'll point out again that under the FairTax visitors to our shores would, for the first time, be contributing to the cost of these two programs. Right now, Social Security and Medicare are wholly dependent on payroll taxes from working Americans. Every time a tourist puts down a dollar for a Coney Island Red, a fancy New York City hotel, a rental car in Des Moines, or a funnel cake at a Florida fair, that visitor would be putting money into Social Security and Medicare. Let's free Americans from the tyranny of the IRS and start America's great job-generating machine working at full force; then the matter of reforming Social Security may become more politically palatable.

I'm living on my retirement income. I paid income tax when I earned that money; why should I pay a national sales tax when I spend it?

That's an excellent question, and we sympathize with those who feel the FairTax victimizes them by taxing consumption dollars that were already taxed when they were earned. Do you get as good a deal as current workers, especially the poor? No, you don't. There's nothing we can do to change the fact that the dollars you are spending today were already ravaged by the income tax and payroll taxes. (By the way, the situation is the same for virtually everyone with a savings account.)

Having said that, you will benefit from the FairTax in two separate ways. For one thing, the items you will be purchasing with your already-taxed retirement savings will be, on the average, about 22 percent less expensive than they were before the FairTax. This all but wipes out the effect of the 23 percent national retail sales tax. For another, your retirement income will now be subsidized by your monthly check from the federal government, reimbursing you for the sales tax you'd be expected to pay during that month on the basic necessities of life. And finally, what do you think will happen to your nest egg if all the world's investors can invest in our economy with no tax consequences? You're bound to come out ahead. Younger workers, such as your grandchildren, may do better, but you'll be doing just fine. Make them buy you a new car.

Will the Internet be taxed?

The same principle that determines the collection of taxes on services applies to Internet sales. While we agree with Congress's law forbidding government from taxing *access* to the Internet, we believe that the only fair way to handle sales conducted over the Internet is to tax them in just the same way as any other sale of goods or services. As we've said over and over, government ought to be neutral—period. No retailer who pays taxes in our community ought to be put at a 7 percent disadvantage to some Internet retailer, large or small.

We envision a department of the Treasury to deal with Internet and catalog sales, with stiff penalties for those selling into our communities who do not abide by the law.

When this first came up several years ago, some objected that forcing catalog or Internet retailers to know the city, county, and state sales tax rates for the entire country would place an unfair burden on the retailers. In fact, Sears, Roebuck—and plenty of other catalog retailers—have been doing this for longer than we can remember.

One group we expect to support the FairTax idea on this score is the nation's governors—since their state economies collectively lost more than $20 billion in revenues last year to Internet and catalog sales they were powerless to tax.

I've been saving to send my children to college. Will their education costs be taxed?

The creators of the FairTax Plan recognize that education is an investment, and thus qualitatively different from a retail purchase of goods or services. So this is another piece of good news: Whether you're trying to get your child—or yourself, for that matter—into a private school, college, or university, the tuition will not be taxed under the Fair-Tax Plan.

If this sounds like a short-term loss to the government, it's also a long-term gain: After all, the more educated you are, the more you'll earn. The more you earn, the more you'll spend. And the more you spend, the more taxes you will contribute to the federal government.

Okay, I'm convinced. What can I do to help get this FairTax thing passed?

Turn the page.

16

OKAY. GREAT IDEA.
SO WHAT DO WE DO NOW?

In our travels promoting the FairTax, we've run into more than a few people who have studied the material, embraced the idea, but can't bring themselves to imagine the FairTax becoming law. To them it seems just too good to be true—or, more to the point, too good to make it through the halls of Congress. In fact, this may be the biggest single concern we hear about the prospect of the FairTax: "Well, it's a great idea, but it'll never happen. Congress would never pass it."

Are you prepared to just walk away and accept that kind of defeatism? After reading this book, and considering what the FairTax would mean to you personally, to your children, and to this country, are you prepared to shrug it all off with a simple "Nice try, but we'll never get this passed"?

It's been said that anything the mind of humanity can envision humanity can accomplish. More than 225 years ago, the minds of certain individuals were envisioning an America free and independent of British tyranny. Doubters? You bet there were doubters! When the battle was first engaged on Bunker Hill, the majority of colonists were dead set against the idea of American independence—mostly because they thought the battle would be terrible and virtually impossible to win. Today, most of us are rather pleased that the battle was joined nonetheless.[1]

There is a lot of behind-the-scenes support for the FairTax in Washington. Some of it is quite visible, some more covert. The politician coauthor has presented the concept of the Fair-Tax to virtually all of those whom we would call "movers and shakers" in Washington. Some are willing to lend their immediate support. Others are more cautious. Most, however, think the basic idea is wonderful. Just last year, after being briefed on the FairTax, one cabinet-level official exclaimed, "This is incredible! Why haven't you passed it yet?" A typical FairTax conversation with an elected official might sound something like this: "Look, Congressman Linder, I think this FairTax idea is superb. Obviously it will work, and it will bring unprecedented economic growth. I want to support it, I really do, but I just can't lend my name to the effort until I see it's going to have widespread support from the public. I'm facing a pretty tough reelection next year, and I have to

---

1. That would be most of us outside the halls of academia.

be careful about giving my opponent any ammunition to use against me."

It's just a political reality: There are many officials in Washington, elected and otherwise, who like the FairTax proposal, but even today they are holding back to wait for a groundswell of support among their constituents. As soon as they see that growing surge of support, they will join in and use it to help pass the FairTax Act.

That's where *you* come in. Inertia is everything in Washington, and the present income tax system has some massive inertia going for it. It won't be turned on a whim. The Fair-Tax represents such a fundamental change in the way Washington does business that it stands virtually no chance unless Beltway politicians know that the American public is behind this change. For all but a few members of the House and the Senate, Job One is always to get reelected. They're not going to jeopardize their reelection chances by signing on to a piece of admittedly radical legislation without knowing in advance that their constituents are behind them.

What we're saying, in other words, is that it's pretty much up to you.

Our current income tax plan was designed by politicians; as such, it was designed to benefit politicians and serve their ends. Frank Chodorov, one of America's past champions of liberty, once observed that, by enacting the income tax, the American government was proclaiming that all wealth belonged to the government, and whatever wealth the government did not seize from the person who created it should be looked on as a concession—a gift from the government.

The FairTax was designed by economists and researchers at the best American universities, with help from some of America's most accomplished businesspeople. As such, it was designed to benefit the American free enterprise system and to promote economic liberty. There is nothing coercive about the FairTax. Under its provisions, each and every family in America can meet its basic needs with no federal tax consequences at all. It is only when you choose to spend above the level of basic necessity that you begin to pay any taxes to support the operation of the federal government.

In short . . . income taxes are seized. Consumption taxes are paid. Which way do you want it?

Deciding whether or not you want to get behind the Fair-Tax Plan may involve coming to an understanding of your view of America.

Do you consider America a great country? If so, why? Do you believe that America is great because of its government, as so many politicians do; or do you believe we're a great country because of the dynamic energy that flows from a free people operating under the rule of law as they pursue their personal interests under a system of economic liberty? Make your choice. If you believe that America is great because of its government, then we'll admit that the FairTax may not be for you. If you believe in the dynamic of freedom and economic liberty, on the other hand, you'll probably recognize just how good the FairTax proposal is.

If politics has been little more than a spectator sport for you up until now, it's time to change. It's time for you to be a player, not just an observer. The FairTax can become law . . . but *only* if the people of this country let their elected representatives know they *want* it to become law. It really is up to you. As this book is being printed, the FairTax legislation is before the House Ways and Means Committee. Coauthor John Linder is a member of that Committee and will eagerly report any groundswell of support for the FairTax to the other members. But there must be a groundswell to report.

That groundswell can be created by you. Talk the FairTax up to your neighbors. Write letters to the editors; call radio and television talk shows. Offer to write an op-ed piece for your local newspaper or neighborhood newsletter. Keep a sharp eye and ear tuned for pundits, talk show hosts, and, yes, politicians who misrepresent the FairTax principle . . . and then step forward to correct the record.

Okay . . . if you're with us, here's your first step: Pay a visit to www.fairtax.org, the website for Americans for Fair Taxation, which remains the principal organization fighting for passage of the FairTax. With just a few mouse clicks, you can join the FairTax.org e-mail list, sign a petition in support of the FairTax, drop a line to your representatives in Washington, become a FairTax volunteer, and answer any questions you may have about the FairTax. Oh, and you can also contribute to the cause. Radio and television commercials and the materials needed to keep the FairTax in front of our elected officials aren't free. Fairtax.org also keeps a scorecard tracking which senators and congressmen support the FairTax, and which do not. There's also a list of cosponsors. Bookmark the site on your computer, and come back often to get the latest news on the status of H.R. 25.

After you've joined forces with FairTax.org, you can make your presence known to your senators and congressmen. The

FairTax website will let you know if your elected representatives are supporters or not. If you find they already support the FairTax, write them a brief letter letting them know you're behind them. If they don't support the FairTax, you might write to ask them why. If they respond by claiming, as several have, that the FairTax would be especially rough on low- and middle-income Americans, write them back and suggest that they actually read the bill.

Now . . . a word about just how to contact your senators and congressmen. The more effort you put into your communication (within reason), the more your input is going to be valued. Phone calls are easy. A call to the district or Washington office does count, but not all that much. An e-mail carries a little more weight. Letters lead the pecking order. Be careful, though, not to make those letters long and off-putting. Make them short, neatly written, and courteous. Tell them you've studied the FairTax, and that you want them to do the same. Tell them you believe this revolutionary legislation will transform our nation and our economy. Let them know that the FairTax is important to your business, your family, and your children; and that you want them to give the proposal their full attention and effort.

If you really want to make an impression, show up at a politician's town hall meeting. They know that if you've gone through the trouble to put other activities aside to visit them in person, then you must be serious about your particular cause.

Now is as good a time as any to address the subject of negativism.

Naysayers—every organization has at least one—are the characters who sit on the sidelines and wait for someone else to come up with the good ideas—business plans, marketing ideas, whatever they may be. As soon as the new plan is on the table, the naysayer starts bringing up all the reasons it just can't be done. Why is it that some people get so much satisfaction out of shooting down other folks' ideas? Is it because they have none of their own?

So it is with the FairTax. When radio listeners learned that Neal Boortz had teamed up with Congressman John Linder to write a book on the subject, Boortz's radio show quickly became an unofficial clearinghouse for comments, questions, and information about the FairTax. For the most part, the comments were positive, the questions well thought out and provocative. Yet there was always that one class of caller who seemed to want nothing more than to find fault with the idea. "This FairTax idea of yours won't work because blah, blah, blah . . ."

Well, we have a little secret for you. Guess what? The FairTax is not perfect. Try as they might, the researchers, economists, and financial experts who developed the FairTax Plan just couldn't come up with an idea that was any more flawless than the human beings whose taxes it will collect. Sure, people will try to cheat. Always have, always will. Sure, politicians might try to raise the rate. They can do that now, as we've seen. Sure, some Washington K Street lobbyists and lawyers may have to find another way to make such a lucrative living. Welcome to the real world!

Still, we think you'll agree that this plan to fund the cost of government is far and away better than our current system, based as it is on the principles of overt wealth confiscation and class warfare. There's a reason, friends, that Karl Marx listed a progressive income tax as one of the essentials for a totalitarian society. We gave the income tax a try, and it proved wanting. It's become a tool for politicians to use in bludgeoning their political enemies and rewarding their allies. In fact, it's become the principal tool of class warfare in America. All efforts at reform have failed. The income tax punishes incentive and achievement and rewards those who know the ropes inside the Beltway. The FairTax will have none of these flaws.

Those who are willing to accept second best end up in second place. America is better than that. America is better than the income tax.

It's time for a second American revolution—a tax revolt. Will you be on the front lines?

AFTERWORD

First, a confession: In the winter of 2005–06, as we were rudely ignoring friends and family while writing *The FairTax Book,* we never, not for a minute, realized what we had in store for us. For years—make that decades—we had both been studying and promoting the idea of replacing our torturous income tax system with a consumption tax. Our purpose in writing *The FairTax Book* was simply to put what we had learned, and the details of H.R. 25, The FairTax Act, in writing. We wanted a book to explain to interested parties just what the FairTax was all about, and to address objections to the plan. Little did we know what was coming.

On August 11, 2005, ten days after it was released, we learned that *The FairTax Book*—a book about *taxes,* folks—would debut at number one on the *New York Times* bestseller list. Bookstores were telling us that turnouts for book signings exceeded all expectations, in many cases setting records. In some bookstores, first-day sales of *The FairTax Book* exceeded those of the latest Harry Potter tome. Simply put, we had a hit: a completely unexpected and surprising bestseller!

The authors are (hopefully) bright enough to understand that this book did not achieve this incredible success because of our writing brilliance or the marketing savvy of the publisher (though considerable). This book succeeded because it struck a chord with the American people. We Americans are sick to death of the cost and hassle that accompanies the annual tax preparation frenzy. We don't want to starve the government of its funding; we just want to be able to save and invest with no tax consequences. We want a system of taxation that does not punish hard work and doesn't reward lethargy. We want to see the power of economic liberty turned loose for the betterment of all. We don't want to hand over any of our earnings to the federal government until we have paid for our family's basic necessities. We want to see American corporations come back home, and to see the ten trillion American dollars currently invested overseas—safe from our punishing tax code—brought back home to be invested in our domestic economy. Perhaps most important of all, Americans are coming to realize that our current code exists to empower politicians as much as it does to fund government. We want a change.

Now, if you think we were surprised by the success of *The FairTax Book,* you should have seen the reaction inside the DC beltway! For six years the FairTax had been nothing more than a dream of a group called Americans for Fair Taxation (www.FairTax.org) and an obscure Georgia congressman named John Linder. There were some politicians out there willing to give lip service to the FairTax, but only because they felt they had nothing to fear: There was little chance that the system of personal and corporate income taxes that empowered them would ever face the threat of repeal.

Imagine what happened when suddenly that "obscure Georgia congressman" became a number one bestselling author? When suddenly politicians started receiving letters, calls, faxes, and emails—plus multiple copies of this book— from constituents who want to see this plan become law?

AFTERWORD

It's amazing how quickly things can change.

Still, there will always be skeptics. So in preparing for this new edition of *The FairTax Book,* we wanted to take a moment to respond to the critiques of H.R. 25 we've heard in the last several months. Most of these came from two camps: politicians, many of whom are concerned about a bill that would constitute the greatest transfer of power from government to the people since our country was formed; and K Street lobbyists, who rightly fear that they'd be in for a massive loss of income to their own bottom lines once they no longer have a tax code to manipulate for the benefit of their clients. Supporters of H.R. 25 have sent us literally hundreds of communiqués detailing their reactions to the FairTax; we've also collected hundreds of articles in praise of and condemning the idea. These letters and articles have shown us where the greatest concerns are—and now we get a chance to respond.

To those who come to praise the FairTax, we salute you. To those who come to bury it, read on. Who knows, we could change your mind!

Before we get into the nitty-gritty, let us first offer a few words of surprise at a tactic we never expected when this book was first published. We knew, as you've already read, that those K Street lobbyists weren't going to like this idea at all. These are people who have made a mighty handsome living off our current convoluted tax code. They know that this type of tax reform would quickly send them into another line of work; fighting to defeat the FairTax means fighting for their livelihood.

What we frankly didn't predict was the amazing defensiveness we've seen from so many elected officials. It has now become clear that many of those who are supposed to be serving the people in Washington are actually far more concerned about preserving the powers that come with their jobs—including the power to monkey with our tax code for the benefit of favored constituents and huge campaign donors—than they are with serving the public. As we read through the objections to the FairTax presented by these politicians, one interesting trend quickly became clear: In order for them to come up with a believable reason to oppose H.R. 25, they had to misrepresent its terms. Have a look, and you'll see what we mean.

Several congressmen wrote their constituents with the following argument: Since H.R. 25 doesn't repeal the 16th Amendment, they contended, passing it would leave us with both a sales tax and an income tax.

Well, at least we agree on one thing: The very last thing we would ever want is a combination of a national retail sales tax *and* an income tax. Clearly the 16th Amendment must be repealed. But a Constitutional amendment can only be repealed by a Constitutional amendment, and to send such an amendment to the states for ratification would take a two-thirds vote of both houses of Congress. So, if such an amendment were included within H.R. 25, it would take that two-thirds vote to pass.

But here's what these opponents are glossing over: H.R. 25 may not in and of itself repeal the 16th Amendment, but it *does* repeal Subchapters A, B, C, and H of the 1986 IRS code—that is, the very language that implements the income tax. Once the FairTax law is passed, in other words, the income tax is dead. Could it be brought back to life by politicians? Sure, in theory. But with the popularity of the FairTax, what politician is going to introduce legislation bringing the income tax back? An alternate plan could be to pass the Fair-Tax with a normal majority vote, and then condition the implementation of the tax upon the ratification of a new amendment repealing the 16th Amendment.

However we get there, one thing is clear: The FairTax kicks in only after the income tax leaves off.

Another group of politicians will tell you that that Linder and Boortz are pulling a fast one. The real FairTax rate, they say, is 30 percent, not 23 percent.

We've already covered this in our original chapter 15, "Questions and Objections." It's very simple: Our present federal income tax is quoted on an inclusive basis. We're replacing the income tax with the sales tax, so we quote the sales tax on an inclusive basis as well. You spend $100 and $23 goes to the federal government. The FairTax replaces the cost of the embedded tax in our goods and services caused by our current tax code. We've run the calculations over and over, and $23 out of $100 comes out to 23 percent, not 30 percent, every time. We understand why opponents to this plan would like to quote a higher exclusive tax rate for an inclusive tax. What we don't understand is why they aren't quite so fond of quoting our income tax the same way.

A number of congressmen wrote their constituents to warn them that the FairTax would make everything 23 percent more expensive. Some of them, of course, used the 30 percent figure.

If your elected representatives have given you this line, you know that either they haven't studied the issue, or they've decided, for whatever reason, to intentionally mislead you. The FairTax replaces the embedded tax in all goods or services you purchase at the retail level. It is an "instead of" tax, not an "in addition to" tax. So, when you hear some elected official trying to claim that a $15,000 automobile will now go for $18,000 or $20,000, ask them this: "Congressman So-and-so, are you misrepresenting the effect of the FairTax because you haven't read the bill, or because you're concerned about handing so much power back to the taxpayers?" That ought to go over well.

We have seen numerous letters from congressmen and senators who claim that the FairTax would increase the tax burden on the poor and the middle class—that the FairTax is "regressive."

When people who have actually read this book—or who understand the terms of H.R. 25—hear this argument, they just sigh and shake their heads. The truth is that the FairTax completely *lifts* the federal tax burden off the backs of the poor, as was noted by President Bush's tax reform commission. Those who barely make enough money to cover the basic necessities for their families will not pay one penny in federal taxes under this plan. In fact, they will be getting a totally free ride on our two largest entitlement programs, Social Security and Medicare. How, pray tell, can it then be said that their tax burden would be increased?

But what about the middle class? some ask. Would the FairTax increase the federal tax burden on middle-income Americans? The FairTax is a consumption tax. Any middle-income Americans who would be hit hard by a consumption tax are already being hit equally hard by the embedded tax that exists today in all of the items and services they consume. The FairTax would merely replace the embedded income taxes, payroll taxes, and compliance costs with an embedded national sales tax—giving concerned taxpayers *more* control over how much money they want to pay, not less.

One more point before we move on to the next oft-heard objection. Since the publication of *The FairTax Book,* and the resulting increased interest in this concept, many of the economists who worked to develop this idea many years ago have come forward with renewed support and new research. One such economist is Dr. Laurence J. Kotlikoff of Boston University. In a recent letter, Kotlikoff specifically addressed the idea that the tax burden would actually increase on working Americans, especially the poor and middle class. To quote directly from Professor Kotlikoff's letter: "The FairTax imposes much lower average taxes on working-age households than does the current system. The FairTax's reduction in average tax rates on the working-age population reflects the broadening of the tax base from what is now primarily a system of labor income taxation to a system that taxes, albeit indirectly, both labor income and existing wealth. Consider, as an example, a single household earning $50,000. The household's average tax rate under the current system is 21.1 percent. It's 16.2 percent under the FairTax."

Many elected officials have written their constituents to tell them that the real FairTax rate would have to be higher—much higher—than 23 percent.

The so-called "real" rates cited by political opponents of the FairTax range from 50 percent to as high as 100 percent of a taxpayer's income. How do these opponents arrive at such outrageous figures? They change the terms of H.R. 25, usually by exempting certain items from the tax. Most commonly they eliminate food and medicine. Others eliminate the taxes on food, clothing, new homes, transportation, medical care, etc.—taxes that would enlarge overall tax revenues and help keep the rates down. Remember, the idea here is to simplify the tax code, not to complicate it. The idea of exemptions to the national sales tax appeals to politicians, lobbyists, and their staffs because the existence of exemptions would give them the room to tinker with the tax code. But the bottom line is that such tinkering is a huge source of power for politicians, wealth for the lobbyists—and trouble for the rest of us.

Retired Americans, or those close to retirement, are concerned that they will be double-taxed on their savings and retirement funds.

We absolutely sympathize with those Americans who have worked long and hard for a rewarding retirement, only to worry that their retirement may somehow be threatened by this new tax plan. Many people have written us with their concern that the value of their retirement funds would suddenly be reduced by the imposition of a national sales tax. You've worked too long and too hard to face this type of fear or uncertainty, so let us put your minds to rest right now: Yes, you will be paying the FairTax on the purchase of all goods and services at the retail level. But hold on! The important thing is that _you won't be paying any more for those items than you're paying right now_. Remember, the embedded taxes in those goods and services will have been removed. The companies and individuals involved with bringing that consumer item or service to you will no longer have a tax burden to pass on to you in their pricing structure. The taxes and tax compliance costs they would have passed on to you are simply replaced by the FairTax! So that sailboat or motor home you've been looking forward to will cost pretty much the same under the FairTax as it would cost under today's tax code.

And that's just the beginning! Under the FairTax plan, the earnings on your investment accounts and Social Security benefits will no longer be taxed—so that means you'll have *more* money in your pockets, not less. And don't forget the monthly prebate. Whether you're retired or working, if you're the head of a household you'll still get that check every month to cover all of the federal sales taxes you'll pay during that month on your spending, right up to the poverty line. So, on final analysis, you're coming out on top with the FairTax.

A few members of Congress have tried describing the FairTax as a "hidden tax"—claiming that it would hide how much tax we pay when we buy things.

This one is easy. The fact is, it's our *current* system that does a magnificent job of hiding the taxes you pay. First, as we pointed out earlier, the system of tax withholding masks how much of your paycheck is lost to the federal government. Most Americans think of their income only in terms of "take-home pay." Second, the embedded taxes go completely unnoticed by the majority of consumers. Once the FairTax is implemented, the amount of federal sales tax you've paid will be clearly shown on your receipt. When you purchase a $100 widget, the cashier will hand you a receipt that says "Widget . . . $77. FairTax . . . $23. Total . . . $100."

Now that we think about it, can you imagine how easily we could pass and implement the FairTax if today's receipts read "Widget . . . $78. Embedded federal tax costs . . . $22. Total . . . $100"? Yeah— like that's going to happen anytime soon . . .

There have been quite a few claims, generally from columnists and other pundits, that the FairTax is a right-wing Republican bill.

Yes, believe it or not, we've seen quite a few critiques of the FairTax based entirely on the idea that it's some sort of a right-wing plot against America's poor. Well, if you can't find a factual or logical basis upon which to oppose the Fair-Tax, we guess this will do. One question, though: Since when did removing the poor in our society from any responsibility for paying any federal taxes whatsoever—including Social Security and Medicare taxes—become a part of the right-wing agenda?

This isn't about left or right, Republican or Democrats. The FairTax is about helping lower-income earners save and invest without tax consequences, enabling them to become higher-income earners. The FairTax is about allowing businessmen and women do what they do best, grow and expand their businesses, without concerns over the tax implications of their actions. The FairTax is about making America the world's largest business tax haven, and bringing American businesses, jobs, and capital back home. The FairTax is about expanding job opportunities here at home. If these are right-wing conservative values, then we have to ask: *What's wrong with that?*

One more thing. For generations, the left has been trying to find ways to add a wealth tax on top of our current income tax. During the early years of the Clinton administration, there was some attention paid to the idea of imposing a one-time 15 percent tax on the outstanding balance of all existent pension and 401K retirement plans. The idea died when the Republicans gained control of Congress. With the FairTax, the liberals will have accomplished much of their goal. As things are now, wealthy Americans with no current income have no income tax bill to pay. We can cite many examples of "wealthy" Americans who use their money to purchase tax-free municipal bonds—and then pay no income taxes and no payroll taxes, because they have no taxable income! With the FairTax, these wealthy Americans will be taxed *every time they make a purchase*. Taxing wealth hardly seems like a right-wing Republican idea, now does it?

Many opponents of the FairTax cite widespread fraud as their primary concern. Too many people, they claim, would try to find ways to avoid the tax.

They're absolutely right. Just as in any other system, there will always be people who will try to find ways to avoid paying the tax. What's different is that they'll find it quite a bit *more* difficult to cheat on the FairTax than under the current income tax. Professor Kotlikoff has also addressed this question. Kotlikoff points out that most of the sales of goods and services, and virtually all of the retails sales of expensive goods and services, will be handled in retail stores. These stores aren't going to risk the penalties that go with attempts to avoid the FairTax.

And Professor Kotlikoff makes one more interesting point: Under our current tax code, there are about 140 million "collection points" for the income tax—that is, 140 million American wage earners and businesses. Implement the FairTax, and the number of collection points goes down to about 20 million. The likelihood of a tax cheat being caught are quite a bit higher if you cut the number of tax collection points by about 86 percent.

AND, FINALLY, A WORD ABOUT WEALTH ENVY

What, you might ask, does wealth envy have to do with passage and implementation of the FairTax? Quite a bit. As we've already seen, wealth envy played a huge part in getting the states to ratify the 16th Amendment. People were convinced that this tax would be paid only by rich people from the Northeast, and this was just fine with them.

Wealth envy is as old as civilization. There have always been, and will always be, people who wallow in envy of those who have more. Studies have even shown that people will take actions to harm their own economic well-being if those actions have the effect of punishing the wealthy. Politicians have long been aware of this undercurrent of jealousy, and have become adept at converting envy to votes. In recent years you've heard the phrase "richest one percent" countless times from politicians trying to earn votes through this time-honored means of exploiting jealousy.

This brings us to a major reason many politicians aren't rushing to support the FairTax. Under the new plan, any lingering complaints about the rich not "paying their fair share" will begin to fall on deaf ears among the poor and middle class—as soon as they realize that it allows them to cover their basic necessities with virtually no federal tax burden, while upper income Americans are paying the FairTax on every purchase they make . . . including all those mansions, expensive cars, and private yachts.

Under the FairTax, Beltway denizens will lose their ability to manipulate the federal tax code to exploit hard feelings between economic classes. No longer will political candidates be able to promise voters that they will cut taxes on the poor and raise taxes on corporations and the rich. There will be one FairTax rate, and that rate will be paid by everyone, whatever purchases they make. Each household will receive the prebate, and thus will be protected from the cost of the FairTax on life's basic necessities. The FairTax can't be raised on one segment of the population and reduced on another. Any attempt our elected officials should make to change the FairTax rate would affect each and every household, not just the rich, the poor, or the middle class. Instead of focusing on how much the government is getting from which socioeconomic demographic, the focus could finally switch to a subject we should have been thinking more about all along: just what the government is getting with the money it collects. Americans across the economic game board will realize that controlling the size and the cost of government will have a direct effect on the size of the Fair-Tax they pay. Americans will be united in their attention to what is going on in Washington instead of divided by their economic and tax rate bickering among themselves.

Perhaps we can sum things up this way:

The FairTax would constitute the biggest transfer of power from politicians to the people since the beginning of this country.

Politicians don't give power away. It has to be taken from them. Politicians won't rush to implement real tax reform unless the people absolutely demand it of them.

This can be done. It is not a pipe dream. In addition to H.R. 25 and S. 25, other bills have been introduced in both houses of Congress to repeal our current tax code. A bill currently offered in the House would repeal the tax code by December 31, 2009, and calls for Congress to approve a new federal tax code by July 2009. You may be surprised to know that such bills have been passed on two occasions by the House: first in 1998 and again in 2000. Legislation such as this would have the effect of holding congressional feet to the fire, perhaps leading to a full consideration of the FairTax.

There is a certain inevitability to this. One way or the other, America is destined to change from an income-based system for raising revenues to a consumption-based system. The current system of taxation is careening out of control. Change will come, either out of chaos or by design.

In a recently completed study, the federal government's General Accountability Office concluded that if we continue to tax our overall economy at the current levels—and if federal discretionary spending continues at its current percentage of the overall economy—in just thirty-four years we'll reach the point where the entire federal revenue stream won't be enough to pay the interest on the debt. To ignore this is not just irresponsible, it is criminal.

Sure, we could just raise taxes, but history shows that this would slow the growth of the economy, thus making our situation worse. Should we try to slow spending growth? Sure— but we've seen the congressional track record on that idea, haven't we? The only solution that really makes sense is to change the method of raising revenue for the federal government—to find a way to raise revenue that would bring about economic growth and new sources of revenue. This is exactly what we propose to do with the FairTax.

Right now, we have options. We're being driven by economic realities toward substantive reform in our tax system. There's a fork in the road ahead; one way leads to chaos, the other to orderly change. We need to make the choice, and time is running out. There are five basic economic forces driving us toward reform, all of which have been covered in this book. Before we close, let's take a quick review:

1. We have written at length of the 22 percent tax component in the price system that makes us less than competitive in the global economy. Jobs are moving offshore into nations that have a lower tax on capital and labor.

2. According to the Tax Foundation's most recent report, last year we spent $265 billion filling out IRS paperwork; in ten years, it predicts, we will spend $483 billion annually. Add to that the $100 billion or so that we spend calculating the tax implications of business decisions. That's quite a tab. Eliminating the income tax, and thus those costs, would create the largest virtual tax cut and economic stimulus in the history of the Earth.

3. Our current tax system has delivered to us an underground economy somewhere in the range of $2 to $3 trillion a year—a number that's only growing year to

year, and that does nothing to help defray the costs of our government.

4. Our current tax code has chased roughly $10 trillion in dollar-denominated deposits into offshore financial centers. This is money that wants to be in dollars for safety, but is hiding offshore for secrecy. Without an IRS, that money would be in American deposits and investments. Bringing that money back home to work in our economy would lead to a measurable increase in the value of the American markets, would make most corporate pension funds whole, and end many of the corporate bankruptcies that have become all too common.

5. The FairTax would change the way we fund Social Security and Medicare, from taxing 158 million workers to taxing 300 million citizens and 50 million tourists. This would double Social Security and Medicare revenues in fifteen years by doubling the size of our economy. Crisis over.

None of the above issues will be helped by nibbling around the edges of the current income based tax system. They can only be fixed by moving to a consumption-based tax system like the FairTax. We know this, you know this, and our elected leaders know this. The question, then, is whether we all have the will to work for this goal. Will you join a volunteer group promoting the FairTax? Will you work to educate your representatives and senators? Will you bring the message of the FairTax to your neighbors and colleagues?

Chaos or order? The choice should be easy.

ACKNOWLEDGMENTS

First, we would like to acknowledge our families, who have not only put up with our decades of passion on this issue, but who have also endured our recent collaboration. Our wives, in particular, have provided us in this project—as in life—unlimited support and inspiration.

We want to thank Congressman Collin Peterson of Minnesota, a CPA and Democrat whose original support of the FairTax was critical to its legislative launch. We also want to thank House Majority Leader Tom DeLay, whose support was decisive in putting the FairTax on the legislative map, and whose support today is critical as we push this bill toward the legislative finish line.

We also want thank President George W. Bush and House Speaker Dennis Hastert, both of whom have not only given a nod of understanding to the FairTax, but who have also worked tirelessly to create a political landscape that allows for the passage of big ideas like this one.

Next, we need to acknowledge the extraordinary efforts of Americans for Fair Taxation (FairTax.org). This group not only brought form and structure to this idea we have talked about for so long, but also continues to build grassroots support for the FairTax every day. We thank FairTax.org for sharing its work with us, and we thank the people of FairTax.org for working tirelessly to make this legislation a reality.

In particular, we acknowledge Tom Wright, the executive director of FairTax.org, who believes in the power of FairTax and has spent year after year leading this effort down the political playing field. Tom, as you know, we are as close to the finish line as we have ever been, and your efforts have made that possible.

We also want to acknowledge the Tax Foundation and its president, Scott Moody. The Tax Foundation does very serious and important tax research—work no other organization has taken on. It is difficult, in fact, to discuss tax compliance costs or tax code complexity without citing the Tax Foundation, because its work so dominates the field. To the Tax Foundation, we say thank you for your otherwise thankless work.

The authors also want to acknowledge the hard work of Rob Woodall, who provided invaluable assistance to the authors by spending endless hours researching and fact-checking the points made in this book.

Finally, we want to acknowledge the hundreds of thousands of volunteers in the FairTax.org organization—volunteers who have spent time and money generously to move this idea forward. Some speak at local meetings; some travel across the country to speak where needed. These men and women never ask, "What does the FairTax do for me?" but rather "What will the FairTax do for America?" knowing that what is good for America will be good for them. FairTax cannot become law without this kind of citizen involvement, and we have written this book to help that effort.

INDEX